A Long Way From Beatty

A Long Way From Beatty

A Memoir of Don Smailes

KELLY SMAILES

KELLY SMAILES
EDMONTON, ALBERTA, CANADA

A LONG WAY FROM BEATTY
A MEMOIR OF DON SMAILES

Published by Kelly Smailes, Edmonton, Canada

ISBN 0-978-1-77354-545-5

Publication assistance and digital printing in Canada by

PUBLISHING
PageMasterPublishing.ca

Contents

Author's Note

Have you met my dad? You would remember him if you had. A quick smile, firm handshake or hug, and a ready story if you had time for a chat. After a short time, you would feel you had known him all your life. His has been a full life—knowing poverty and abundance, love, conflict, hard work, and adventure.

I hope you will enjoy reading the following pages as much as I have enjoyed writing them. Names and some details have been changed to safeguard the privacy of those whose lives intersected with Don Smailes and his family. Note that to differentiate brother Gerald Smailes from wife Geraldine Smailes, brother Gerald is called "Jerry" while Geraldine is called "Gerry" (or "Deany" in her younger years).

The story is told in the first person from Don Smailes's point of view as he told it to me. I have endeavoured to fact check, but there will undoubtedly be some errors. If you remember things differently, please know that we are not trying to rewrite history. Sometimes storytellers get carried away!

1. Beginnings

I made my exuberant entrance into this world on July 30th of 1938. Some might speculate that my arrival in 1938 and the beginning of the Second World War in 1939 was suspicious, but I firmly maintain that the war was not my fault. I joined a family of five: parents John and Madge Smailes, brother Gerald, and sisters Phyllis and Patricia living in Prince Albert, Saskatchewan. As with many stories, mine began before my birth, so perhaps we should start there.

Grandparents Clarence and Ida Pearl came to Canada in 1905 from Grey Eagle, Minnesota, because there was land available. They started a farm, and Clarence found work preparing the railroad bed near Webb, Saskatchewan. He would drive teams of six to twelve horses, and there was lots of work to be had with the building of the railway.

Since this seemed like a good opportunity, Clarence arranged for his family to join him and immigrate to Canada. Clarence convinced his dad, Grandpa Pete, to give up his homestead, and they settled in the Admiral, Saskatchewan, area. They didn't own the land but had what was called a preemption and worked for other people. They started a cattle farm there and became the dairy suppliers for that area.

Clarence's wife, Ida Pearl, was afflicted with several health issues, and the family needed extra help to run the dairy. That is how John Smailes, my father, came to work for them as a farmhand.

Madge, my mother-to-be, had completed her Grade 12 as well as normal school which is what they used to call Teachers' College. She wanted to become a teacher and was engaged to a man in the community. Story has it that John made a bet that he could win her away from that person. John Smailes was quite charismatic and a good storyteller. I don't know how handsome he was, but charm and charisma are often more effective than looks when it comes to sweeping a girl off her feet!

John took on the task of winning Madge's heart and, before too long, she was discovered to be pregnant with his child. This caused quite a dilemma in the family. They were faced with the decision of whether to send Madge back to Minnesota to have the baby and give it up for adoption, or have her marry this scoundrel and keep the child. The decision was made for them to marry. They wed in November of 1931, and Phyllis Irene came along some months later in May of 1932.

Madge and John were obviously in love, and the physical expression of that love meant that babies arrived almost every year or two. This was before the days of contraceptives, so their second child, James, was born a year after Phyllis in 1933. The birth was a very difficult one, and complications meant that James did not survive.

John and Madge comforted each other on the loss of this tiny life not yet begun. A year later, in November of 1934, Gerald was born. There were complications with his birth too; he was in a breach position and was delivered with a broken arm, but otherwise robust and healthy.

Two years later in July of 1936, Patricia joined the family, and in July of 1938, I was born.

There is not a lot of information about how this young family made ends meet in the early days. We had left the Pearl family farm, and there was some moving around as Dad worked at various jobs. When I was born in Prince Albert, my father was employed as a butcher at the slaughterhouse.

The Second World War happening a continent away changed everything in our family. Dad terminated his employment in Prince Albert with the start of the war in 1939 and disappeared. After some investigating, Mom found out that that he had, like many abled-bodied men of that time, signed up for the Canadian Army and was in Ontario preparing to go overseas. When she went down to the Armed Forces offices, she made the further discovery that he had signed up as a single man. Mom informed the army that twenty-nine-year-old John Smailes was, in fact, her husband and the father of their four children. With that straightened out, the family would have some financial support from Dad's military pay.

In 1940, Dad left Canada to spend the next five years in Europe with the Canadian Army. The little Smailes family moved from Prince Albert to Shaunavon, Saskatchewan, to be nearer Mom's family.

Madge and children on the Buckingham farm in Admiral, SK

2. Shaunavon, 1940-1946

My memories of Shaunavon are good memories; we were a happy family. Of course, we were sad not to have Dad present, but Mom was the centre of our home, and she was amazing. She cared for us and was such a good mom that we rarely felt the absence of anything vital even during such a time of upheaval in the world. We were always fed, clothed, and loved. In retrospect, Mom's desire to be a teacher probably made her especially engaged in reading to us and teaching us as we grew up. I remember her reading Bible stories to us at night and saying bedtime prayers.

Our home was very adequate for the time. It had seven rooms; four upstairs bedrooms meant the boys shared one room, the girls had another, one was a sewing room for Mom, and the fourth was a guest room. Mom's bedroom was on the main floor to the left of the back door. Through her room was the indoor bathroom, and to the right was the living area and kitchen.

We lived only two blocks from the school and close to downtown. Shaunavon was not that big, but we got to see and experience a lot. My earliest memories there were pre-school and the wonderful freedom that afforded me to just be a child. Before Grade 1, I was a dreamy kid with no concept of responsibility or of how hard life could be. As the youngest, I may have been spoiled just a little. My sister Pat remembers me laying on the floor, kicking and screaming while trying to get my own way. I obviously have a strong will, and according to my sister, Mom had a hard time handling me on occasion.

Mom did not believe much in corporal punishment, so we probably got away with some behaviour that was later corrected when Dad came home and introduced us to his authority and enforcement. I remember laying on the floor in front of the gramophone, singing along to the music: "Tell me why my daddy don't come home . . ."[1]

There was certainly a loneliness there and vacancy in our lives without a dad, but it was not paralyzing. It was just our reality; the reality of many families as the war went on.

Shaunavon was a neat little town. We lived near the end of the block in a house that is still standing, though perhaps not habitable today.

One of the best things about our house was that it was next to a vacant lot where all the neighbourhood kids gathered to play. Kick the can, tag, scrub baseball; the possibilities were endless with imagination and a few friends.

Shaunavon also boasted a swimming pool where I learned to swim. It was only a fifteen-minute walk from our house, and we went there regularly. I could swim as far as I could hold my breath and was proud of that accomplishment at only six years of age. There was a lot of splashing and thrashing, with little finesse, but as long as I could stand up on the bottom or on someone or something, I could take a breath. It was a great way to cool down on a hot day.

During the war, we had coupons or tokens that allowed us to buy things that were being rationed. In order to support our troops, we learned to economize and sometimes do without certain items. I remember the little blue tokens had a small hole in them, similar to what we later had for milk delivery. Luxuries like butter and meat were in short supply and could only be bought with these tokens.

Mom worked hard to keep us fed and healthy. One of the rules of the house was that whatever she cooked, you ate. I've always had a good appetite, but there were some things she made that I did not like. Stewed tomatoes!! Why on earth would God make something like a tomato? And why would people think stewing them with all those seeds in them was a good idea? I knew enough from watching things in the garden that plants came from seeds, and I sure didn't want tomato plants to grow out of me! Nonetheless, what Mom said was the rule, and I spent more than one evening sitting at the table counting tomato seeds while the other kids amused themselves outside. Hearing their shouts and laughter as they played right next door made it even harder to face the impossible task of cleaning my plate.

I was an adventurous kid who loved to climb and investigate things. The world was my playground, and I don't recall being afraid of much. That resulted in some scrapes and bruises that Mom patched up on more than one occasion. I still carry the scar from a rake that broke my fall one day while walking on a rickety fence. I think I really wanted to fly, but gravity always won out.

In those days, we didn't go to the hospital for many ailments. We all enjoyed pretty good health; perhaps it was the tomatoes? When the inevitable colds would come, Mom put a blanket over my head and had me breathe the steam from a pot of hot water and Vicks. Perhaps that's where a seed was planted to have me work in respiratory therapy.

Simple home remedies carried us through most of our lives. The only time I remember being in hospital was when I was six years old and my tonsils had to be removed. I have vivid memories of dizziness and the sensation of spiraling down a dark tunnel, while being surrounded by horrible smells. That was not a pleasant experience, and it's rather remarkable that I would end up making my living in healthcare and working in a hospital.

We had good neighbours in Shaunavon. The Hardens lived right next door and had a well with a pump. In the wintertime, they allowed us to make a skating rink which provided lots of fun and more than a few dreams of being the next great Canadian hockey player.

Mr. Harden owned the town's newspaper. I was too young at that time, but my brother Gerald and sister Phyllis both got to work for Mr. Harden delivering the papers. This kept them quite busy since the papers had to be delivered every day after school. Saturday was collection day, and the excitement of getting paid for the week's hard work. Sometimes Jerry would let me come along with him on Saturdays to collect the money from his subscribers. While that was exciting, the real treat was when we would go to the restaurant afterwards to enjoy a slice of raisin pie with ice cream. He really was a great big brother and raisin pie is still a treat!

Jerry was a hard worker. I would almost say he was Mom's favourite, but a little brother's perception might be a bit skewed. Still, he was very responsible and worked hard. He took his paper route seriously and it didn't matter what weather or other circumstances might arise, those papers were delivered. That was expected by his employer, and Jerry had been taught to follow through on his commitments.

One night, Jerry came home from delivering his papers and he was as white as a sheet. Mom noticed his ghostlike appearance and asked what was wrong. Jerry said he had been shot at by someone.

The police investigated, and when they went to the place where Jerry reported being shot at, they found a lock of his hair! They also discovered that a patient from the nearby mental institution had gotten out (whether he'd been released or had escaped, I don't recall), and that was the person who had shot at him with a .22. Jerry was so responsible and stalwart that he finished the rest of his paper route before reporting the incident, even though the bullet had come close enough to "part his hair" in essence.

Jerry was already in Grade 4 or 5 and had lots of friends from school. They built a clubhouse at the end of our block, and on occasion this little brother was allowed to go into their treehouse. It was a special treat to get to climb the ladder and hang out with the big kids. Climbing the ladder to get into the clubhouse wasn't a problem for me; keeping me from climbing was more of an issue! But Jerry was a good big brother and allowed me to tag along.

It was in Shaunavon that my attraction to nature began. I remember a golf course just south of our house that afforded some great opportunities for exploring and learning about the world. In one of the sand boxes, I found my first mouse nest! There were tiny naked baby mice; they didn't have any fur on them yet. I was fascinated! I don't think those little mice survived my visit since I've always been more of an adversary to rodents than an advocate, but I sure did enjoy finding them.

Speaking of rodents, did you know that the ground in southern Saskatchewan moves with gophers? They are everywhere!

During the war, our home became infested with bedbugs, and we had to leave the house while it was fumigated. We stayed with our cousins who lived just out of town. I was already going to school at that time, carrying my lunch pail. It was spring and there were a million little gophers everywhere! On my way home from school one day, I was able to harvest six little gophers just by hitting them with my lunch pail. I would run to catch them before they ran down their hole and hit them with my pail. What a great hunter I was!

Since that time, I've often thought that the best kind of exercise for kids is chasing gophers. We would find gopher holes and pour water down the hole to flush them out. The gophers came running out to avoid drowning, and we would chase them. Nothing is more hilarious or dangerous than to give kids a stick and have a half-dozen of them chase the gophers as they come out of the hole. I think the gophers would probably win and you would have a few wounded kids, that's for sure!

Another favourite memory from my childhood was when the fair came to town each year. Never mind the animals, contests, rides, and other activities; I was very good at finding things that people dropped.

A similar bonus happened in the summer when there would be a dance every Saturday night. Of course, I was too young to be interested in the main event, but I would go to these locales the next morning to search the grounds for money and other treasures since something about those activities caused people to drop valuables without noticing. I often look at the ground as I'm walking to this day—perhaps still looking for discarded money or pop cans! I wouldn't recommend this as a habit since you can miss an awful lot of sunsets and sunrises, not to mention opportunities to interact with people if you're always looking at your feet.

One of the benefits and challenges of being the youngest child in the family is that you're motivated to do the things your older siblings do. I was very motivated! My sister remembers that by the age of six, I was riding a bicycle. If I couldn't reach the pedals from the seat, I would perch under the bar. Up and down the street I would fly for hours every day. I loved to run my hand and fingers along the gauge wire fences as I went by since it made a great noise when your fingers went through the spokes of the fence. One day, I got a little too vigorous and lost my thumb nail to the fence. That was a painful lesson.

Sports were a big part of our growing up. Our whole family was very competitive, particularly the boys. I learned to play baseball early on, and the vacant lot beside our house made a perfect ball diamond. We would play five hundred which involved one person batting and the others catching the ball. You would get one hundred points for catching a pop fly, and when you got to five hundred, you would get to be the one batting. This was a great way to develop eye-hand coordination, and even before the age of six, I was an avid player.

Shaunavon had a sports centre about a block away from us where there was a rink. I remember going to hockey games there as a kid. Our team often played against the Notre Dame Hounds from Wilcox, SK. Those were good rivalries between Shaunavon and Wilcox. I was too young to play hockey, but the games were very exciting, and I was an avid fan, longing for the day I could compete too.

During the war, our homes were heated by coal and wood fires. We didn't have all the safety precautions and equipment we have now, and the fire danger was significant. I remember two major fires in Shaunavon while we lived there. The hotel burned down and that was a big fire. Everyone from the town gathered to watch the town lit up for blocks. It was really quite a spectacle!

The other fire was the service station that was kitty- corner from the vacant lot next to our house. I remember the blaze, but mostly I remember that since the service station sold things like chocolates, when these were affected by the fire, we got to eat them. They were the best chocolates I ever had! They were probably the only chocolates I ever had since our family budget didn't have room for such luxuries, but they were really good.

The service station behind us is the one that burned down

During those years, trains were the primary mode of transportation. Delivery in town was done by horses and what we called dray service. If you received something from someone, it usually came on the train. It may have come to the post office, but if it was bulky or heavy, it was delivered by the drayman and his horses.

Because the trains were before diesel automatic mode locomotives, they were powered by coal, and the by- product of that was cinders. The cinders were then used as road covering. We didn't have a lot in terms of material possessions, but we did have shoes. The story is that my mother had a hard time keeping me in shoes. Not that my feet grew quickly, but I would leave my shoes anywhere and everywhere. I much preferred going barefoot and after walking on every surface imaginable, including the sharp cinders on the road, I had feet as tough as those people from India who could walk on fire.

One of our neighbours was a beekeeper, and I was fascinated by that. He would bring some of his hives into Shaunavon to harvest the honey. He had clothing with netting and a special hat to protect his skin from the bees, but the bees really wouldn't bother you if you didn't bother them. I remember him allowing us to have the bees on our hands and they never stung us. I loved learning about how the bees made honey. One day when he didn't have his protective gear on, this neighbour dropped a hive and the bees got upset. He was stung many times and had to be hospitalized because of the toxins from the bee stings. It was a lesson to me that things you think are safe, can become dangerous if you have an accident.

Mother's job was primarily mothering; with four kids ranging from age three to age nine, she was kept busy taking care of us. However, she was also a talented seamstress and sewed special gowns for the young girls who were being confirmed in the Catholic church across the street from us. Having this extra source of income was helpful to make Dad's military pay stretch during this time.

L-R: Jerry, Pat, Madge, Don, Phyllis in Shaunavon. The Catholic church across from our home is seen in the background.

Mom came to faith during a season of desperate need; having four children to raise during wartime when Dad was overseas brought challenges that took her to the end of her resources and abilities. Mom found a supportive faith community in the Apostolic church, and there met Jesus. She became a woman of prayer and faith, and Sunday mornings found our small family in the little church near the swimming pool. I remember enjoying the singing and wondering at the lively demonstrations of the Spirit's power. There was certainly lots of shaking and hollering. As the youngest, I sat next to Mom and loved playing with the little fox tail on the collar of her coat. Snuggled up next to her, I felt safe and loved.

Apostolic church in Shaunavon, SK

Madge's Sunday school class.

My conversion experience at six years old was a result of conviction that came during a church service. I knew that I needed Jesus, and my mother prayed with me at my bedside when I asked God to forgive me for my sin. I was born into the kingdom of God that day, and my mom was the person God used to bring me into His kingdom.

The life of the church was a big part of our family's journey. Our pastor was a man by the name of Don Scott. The Scott family became our closest friends. They were a great source of strength and encouragement to Mom. They had three girls and a boy, and the parents became our models of what adults should be. They were very good people, and they were part of God's provision for our family during that time.

3. Homecoming

As the war progressed and the Allies were gaining victories in Europe, I remember us receiving telegrams. A messenger came on a scooter to bring the telegram to our house, and we received word that Dad would be coming home. I recall the celebration and excitement when he arrived. Since I was too young to remember much before the war, this was really my first memory of Dad. Everyone was talking at once and laughing as he was divided amongst four kids and a wife that he was certainly very happy to see.

Dad's arrival changed everything. When he came back from the war in 1945, he was thirty-five years old. He had been a trooper with the Canadian Princess Patricia light infantry which meant he was a foot soldier, although he also spent some time in a tank as a gunner. He was in great shape physically, but like many who have experienced the horrors of war, his emotional and mental health were not good.

When Dad returned, he had to get to know his children again, and we were excited to show him what we could do. I remember how he would throw a dime in the swimming pool and watch as I dove off the side to go underwater and get that dime. When I emerged dripping and clutching that little piece of silver in my fist, I felt very proud.

Dad's homecoming changed my understanding of authority. Dad was in charge, and there was no room for debate about his authority. He was the boss of our home. He had a German army belt that he had brought home from the war that became the instrument of punishment if you didn't follow the rules. We kids managed to remove the buckle, which was quite painful, but the belt was still a very effective teacher. I don't remember getting too many spankings since one was often enough to teach the lesson that you'd better not do whatever had earned you a spanking anymore. Later on, when we moved to Beatty, SK, we kids managed to hide the rest of the belt between the floors of the house, and I don't think it was ever found until the house was torn down. It didn't alter the policy of corporal punishment in our home, but at least the instrument of punishment was changed.

Dad's spiritual journey was something we never understood. His faith had a lot of unknowns, and he would not have been considered a devout man. He was not a churchgoer and used alcohol and tobacco which were not part of a Christian life as far as we had been raised to believe. While Dad took the place of authority in our home, Mom still had significant input into the decisions made for our family. She also knew how to handle her husband if he got out of line. Mom didn't allow Dad to use alcohol in our home. I recall at least one occasion when Dad came home drunk, and she made him sit outside on the step drinking coffee until he sobered up. She would not tolerate a person under the influence of alcohol in our house.

Like many kids, I was curious about cigarettes, and the fact that my dad smoked made me think I should try it out for myself. As a six-year-old, I found some discarded cigarette butts and something to light them with, and tried smoking. Hidden in the bushes, I tried to be cool, but the awful taste and coughing fits that followed convinced me this wasn't something I wanted to pursue. Years later as I made my living in respiratory therapy, I was grateful that smoking hadn't become a habit.

4. Beatty 1946-1956, Life on the Farm

When Dad returned from the war, he had to find an occupation. One of the careers he investigated was working with the railway either as an engineer or flagger. When he went for interviews, he discovered that he was colour-blind, so neither of those jobs were an option for him. He found out the government was providing farming opportunities to servicemen through the Veterans' Land Act and went to Beatty where he obtained a half section of farmland. One quarter was in the municipality of Flett Springs and the other was in Kinistino.

Dad went on ahead to start the farm while the rest of our family stayed back in Shaunavon to prepare for the move. I was just finishing Grade 1, and I don't have a lot of memories of the move itself. As a six-year-old, I really had no responsibilities but to coast along with the rest of the family.

When moving day finally arrived, we boarded the train in Shaunavon and went to Melfort, where we were met by our Uncle Clifford and Aunt Lois. Clifford was my mom's younger brother who had been living in Melfort for a year. They picked us up and we made the muddy trip to the farm.

We saw the dingy grey frame house that was to be our home. It was quite different from the home we had in Shaunavon during the war. This house was covered in shiplap and had windows up on the second level as well as a stovepipe coming out of the roof. Dad was there to greet us, but we were still getting to know him, and added to that was the adventure of making a home in this new place.

Jerry, Don, Phyl, and Pat at the farm in Beatty.

It's hard to explain how different this part of Saskatchewan is from the prairies of the Admiral and Shaunavon region where there were very few trees. Beatty was a veritable forest in comparison! The soil was also very different in the Melfort area. It's known as the Carrot River Valley and has three to four feet of very black topsoil that is tremendous for growing and agriculture. It's also rather effective at turning white kids black when they've been out in the field playing.

It was a new chapter for me in understanding animal life. With our limited exposure to farms, and in the town of Shaunavon, we knew a little bit about horses. However, we had never lived out where we used them daily. On the farm, they were part of the way we made our living.

The birds were totally different too. I remember the snipes and shorebirds in the Shaunavon area that congregated around the alkaline pools of water. In Beatty, we were introduced to crows, magpies, hawks, owls, and all kinds of different birds. In the old barn, we discovered groundhogs—little brown animals we had never seen before. When backed into a corner, they could become very aggressive. Of course, we had to antagonize them and satisfy our curiosity about these odd little creatures.

Our farm was very primitive. We didn't have any of the amenities we had enjoyed in Shaunavon. The buildings were old, and we didn't even have a well. There was an old ramshackle barn that needed a bulldozer to put it out of its misery. There were nails sticking out of the old boards in the barn, so I had my first experience of stepping on a rusty nail. Thankfully, Mom had some good nursing skills and understood that rusty nails could lead to infection and perhaps even lockjaw or tetanus. She made up a poultice of cooked oatmeal and onion which was applied to my foot inside a sock. This was meant to pull out the pus and poison. Today's first aid providers would probably scoff at this old remedy, but it was all we had in those days and seemed to be effective.

The old house that we lived in was a two-storey combined building. The nails had been made by pouring iron or steel in a mold. They were square and we had never seen anything like them. The siding was weathered shiplap, and the windows were single pane and didn't fit too well.

The house didn't have a basement, so one of the first things we did was to dig out the soil underneath. We used a big scoop called a Fresno scraper which was pulled by the horses. I don't remember how we did that underneath the house that was sitting on concrete blocks, but I do recall that there were a lot more of those groundhogs under the house that had to be evicted. My dad had a rifle, but I don't think we used it. Chasing the groundhogs with sticks was much more fun.

I remember the first time I saw a crow's nest. I had never seen one before! They use all kinds of sticks to make their nest up in the top of the trees. I climbed up to investigate. I was a pretty good climber and could shinny up the trunk until I reached the branches which provided foot and hand holds. I got up to the nest and took one of the eggs, then climbed back down to show my dad.

"That's a crow egg," he said.

It was the first time I had seen one! Little did I know that those crows would become a good source of pocket money for us. Ducks Unlimited had identified crows and magpies as threats to the duck population. To help mother nature, they offered a bounty for the legs of crows and magpies. You could get five cents for a pair of crow legs and eight cents for a pair of magpie legs. Thus began my early career robbing nests and hunting these nuisance birds.

We had to be innovative since there were few ways to earn money as kids Picking up beer and pop bottles along the roads was one source of income. We had to wash them out because they were always dirty, but we got two cents for them and they were recycled. I'm still known to pick up cans and bottles along the road, and these days they're worth a bit more.

Horsehair was used to make furniture and other things, so we collected that as well. Near our farm and along the road to another farm where Dad was working, you could find a plant called Seneca. We would dig it up, take it home, and wash it. Then Dad would take it to the market to sell to those who made a medicinal extract from the roots.

Our house had no insulation, so we opened up the exterior walls and filled them with wood shavings in preparation for the winter. This provided some protection from the cold. Then we put bales of straw around the outside of the house to keep the wind from going in under the floor. We also removed the shiplap siding and replaced it with a material that came in eighteen- by thirty-six-inch sheets and resembled bricks.

Inside the house there were two rooms on the main floor separated by a doorway. It looked as though two houses had been pushed together and you could see the seam between them. These were our kitchen and living area. There was no central heating; only the kitchen stove and a bookers stove in the living room. These each had a reservoir that was filled with wood or coal which would then feed the stove and provide warmth.

Jerry, Don, Pat, and Phyl in front of the farmhouse in Beatty.

The summer was fine because the weather was warm, but winter was a different story. It was cold!! In order for the heat to get upstairs where we slept, it had to come through the stovepipe or through the hole in the floor above the bookers stove. The biggest challenge was keeping the heat in and the cold out. It's a wonder we didn't burn the house down. In fact, we almost did!

Celebrating our first Christmas in Beatty, we must have still had enough money for presents, because I remember we were burning the wrapping paper in the stove. The stovepipe got red hot all the way up and started the roof of our house on fire. Somehow, Dad got up there to douse the flames with salt so that we didn't burn the house down, but it was quite an experience.

Our main source of fuel for the kitchen stove was wood. Because much of the land was covered with bush, one of our first tasks was to clear that bush for planting. The clearing was done using a big old tractor with a blade on the front that would cut down the trees. The trees then had to have the limbs removed, and the trunks were hauled in by the horses, near the woodpile where they were sawed up to fit the stove.

We would pile up those big trees until we could use the community saw. When that day came, we hooked up the saw to the tractor which turned the big saw blade. We would have two or three people moving the tree into the blade to cut pieces that were between a foot and eighteen inches long so they would fit in the stove. My job was to catch the pieces of wood that were cut off and throw them into a pile in preparation for filling the wood box. The next step was to take an axe and cut the logs up. That was my job as well as taking the cut pieces into the wood box in the house. I did this chore from the age of eight onwards. Often, I had to be reminded to fill the wood box when the indoor supply was getting low. And sometimes if I had gotten into mischief of some kind, going to the woodpile and doing a good job of filling the wood box might get me out of trouble.

I learned how to use an axe and how to chop wood effectively, mostly by trial and error. I'm sure my dad demonstrated how to use the axe at first, but it took some practice to develop finesse and avoid injury. I found that if a stick was too long and you hit it with the axe when it was against another piece of wood, you could have two sticks. If you didn't do it right, the sticks would fly up, and on one occasion I had an errant stick hit me on the cheek, producing a "dimple" that I still have today. Experiences like that taught me to adjust my practice to avoid further injury. We had no face shields or protective equipment, so we learned by trial and error how best to do things without hurting ourselves.

The woodpile was also a place of discipline and correction. One spring when the road was too muddy for the horses to take us to school, we walked the four and a half miles along the railroad tracks. On the way to school, we crossed Goose Hunting Creek. The railway bridge over the creek was so narrow that if you were crossing it and a train came, you would have to jump off into the creek some twenty feet below. Thankfully the trains only came a couple of times each day, so we never had to make that jump.

On my way to school one spring day, I stopped to throw rocks into the creek. You have to appreciate that in Beatty there are no stones in the fields, and the only place to find stones to throw at birds' nests is in the railway bed where they are plentiful. So, I stopped and threw stones in the creek, and when I got to school, it wasn't at nine o'clock when the school day began, but more like 10:30 or even 11 a.m. My sister noticed this and, as sisters sometimes do, she told Dad about my tardiness.

When I got home and went into the house, I was given a butcher knife and told to go and cut a willow. The purpose of this willow was not to add to the woodpile, but to teach me that I shouldn't throw stones in the creek when I'm meant to be in school. On my way to cut the willow, I stopped at the side of the house and my sister Phyllis prayed with me to ask Jesus to forgive me. I'm not sure if I was as interested in God's forgiveness as I was hoping that He would get me out of a spanking. I went and cut the willow, brought it into the house, and God answered my prayer; Dad thought I had learned my lesson and I didn't get spanked.

Don on the railroad tracks near Beatty.

Our wood box was located underneath the stairs inside the house. Because the stove had to be on all the time, and it took quite a few armloads of wood to fill it, this chore kept me busy. Later, we used coal in the stove at night so that by morning there might still be some live embers left. Otherwise, if the fire went out, the water in the washing basin would turn to solid ice. Warm blankets and the body heat of siblings huddled together made sleeping possible in the cold winters. So, we managed as a family.

Although we had to work hard and had few luxuries, we had a lot of fun. Mom knew that her children needed to play as well as work, and on Friday nights we would have pillow fights up at the top of the stairs. They were free-for- all's where whoever had the biggest pillow and whoever survived the longest was declared the winner.

Much of our entertainment was also found in reading stories. We even had a battery-operated radio that received a few stations. We would sit around the living room, the kids laying on the floor and listen to Hockey Night in Canada. We got interested in boxing too, and I remember receiving The Ring magazine as a kid growing up. I knew the ratings of all ten divisions and could list the top ten boxers. We listened to the fights on Friday nights and cheered on the likes of Joe Louis, Max Schmeling, Marcel Cerdan, and Ezzard Charles. We knew them all and they were our heroes. Perhaps there was a connection between Friday night boxing and our pillow fights?

We listened to the Lux Radio Theatre mysteries on the wireless too—there was no shortage of fuel for our imaginations in those programs. Those were good days filled with new experiences that were exciting for an eight- year-old.

Starting on a new farm with old buildings, everything had to be built from scratch. Fortunately, Dad was a pretty good carpenter and, with help from a few neighbours and lots of family sweat equity, the construction was done. The barn took shape and was probably about thirty by fifteen feet. It had a sloped roof made of tongue and groove shiplap.

Leftover scraps of wood became our playthings since we didn't buy toys back in those days. A little piece of two- by-four made a great truck or car. We fashioned toy guns and rifles out of lumber scraps, and found that shingles made great arrows. Using a rubber band with a clothespin as the "trigger" you could put the "arrow" in the groove of the shiplap. When you released the stretched elastic, it propelled the shingle down the groove and it would fly maybe fifty yards. Sometimes it would go so far, you couldn't even find the "arrow" afterwards. I don't think we were ever able to shoot straight enough to hit any targets, but we were awfully lucky that we didn't hit one another with our projectiles since that would have resulted in some serious injury.

After the barn was built, the next project was a brand-new chicken coop. Somehow Dad knew something about chickens, so we got forty-nine barred rock hens. We probably had some roosters too, but I remember the hens since it became my job to collect the eggs. Those hens laid an egg every day, and I can recall one day when we had fifty eggs instead of forty-nine, so one of the hens must've laid two eggs on that particular occasion.

The eggs were collected, cleaned, and graded. Then we sent them away to sell, and that was a source of income for us. The chickens were well looked after—they were free range and so the eggs were really good. Being Barred Rock hens, the eggs had dark brown shells but inside they looked like any other eggs. That was a big part of our first operations on the farm.

Collecting the eggs from the chicken coop and bringing them into the house was best done while there was still daylight since we had no lights in the chicken coop. One evening in the wintertime, I had not collected the eggs when I should have and went into the coop in the dark to gather them. The chicken coop had six or eight little compartments that served as nesting boxes for the hens to lay in. There was a door on the front of each compartment where you could reach in and collect the eggs. I went into the dark coop, lifted up the lid of the first compartment, and felt something furry sitting there. I thought it was a cat and went up to the house to tell my dad that the cat had gotten into the chicken coop.

When I reached the house, the rest of the family wouldn't let me come in. Unbeknown to me, I had put my hand on a skunk that had gotten into the laying boxes, and he didn't appreciate the interruption to his egg feast. He sprayed me, and the smell was so strong that even washing my jacket didn't take away the stink. I've since learned that tomato juice can take away the smell of skunk, but we had no tomato juice. As a result, I stunk all winter and people called me Smelly instead of Smailes.

The other skunk encounter I recall was when skunks had burrowed under our chicken coop. We had some tame ducks we were raising, and one day I discovered that the skunks had apprehended the ducks and dragged them into their burrow. My solution was to shoot the skunks and kill them. However, they managed to spray before they died, and if you go back there today, seventy years later, you may still smell them. Growing up in Saskatchewan, you quickly learn that you shouldn't shoot skunks or threaten them in any way. God has built into them the most pungent perfume you will ever encounter, and they are best left alone.

I remember the first cow we got; her name was Bessie. She was so tame and gentle that both Gerald and Phyllis learned to milk her. This was before the new barn had been constructed, and she would just stand out in the yard with one of them holding her by the halter and the other milking her. When Bessie was milked, she would give about a two-gallon pail full of milk at each milking. We would milk her in the morning and again in the evening.

Jerry milking Bessie while Phyl holds her halter.

The milk was brought up to the house where it was put into the bowl of the cream separator. You turned the crank on the separator and as the milk went through, the cream was spun off the top. We drank the skim milk that resulted from this operation, and the cream was shipped to the creamery for some cash. We also kept some cream to be made into butter.

Our churn consisted of a ceramic crock with a wooden plunger in it. You would plunge it up and down until the cream turned into butter and then you poured off the buttermilk liquid. Some people enjoyed drinking the buttermilk, but to me it was sour, and I never understood why anyone would want to drink that when there was real milk to be had.

Food was never in short supply on the farm. We had chickens, and we raised pigs and beef. It was an exciting time, and we were well cared for. We kids shared in all the chores. One thing that we did together was the dishes. There were always dishes to be washed after every meal, and we had a schedule to keep track of whose turn it was. You could sometimes negotiate a little bit of time off on the schedule if you could trade with somebody, but everyone was expected to do the dishes and some of our best sibling fights happened around dish duty. We weren't allowed to break things, so we were careful about that, but we sure had lots of squabbles around the kitchen. That's where you learn how to snap a wet dish towel so that it creates a welt on the arm or the bottom of a sibling.

Water supply was a real challenge for our farm. In that part of Saskatchewan, wells did not produce good water. Our well had so much mineral in it that you didn't want to use the water for washing, and it was even worse for drinking. Our animals didn't like it either, but that's what you got when you dug a well there. So, most people hauled water from nearby creeks and dugouts. We hauled our water about three-quarters of a mile from the creek in a barrel on a stoneboat. We hauled it with horses to start with and then with a tractor and that's what we used to wash clothes. We caught rainwater off the roof for cooking and drinking.

Our washing machine was unique. These days, you can see similar models in museums. It was just a tub with soap particles in it and a handle that moved back and forth to move the clothes around in the water. Soap and water got the dirt out of the clothes, and then there was a wringer attachment that you ran the clothes through to get rid of the excess water. Our dryer consisted of clothes pins and a clothesline where the sun and wind did the job. There was no such thing as an electric dryer.

In fact, we had no electricity for the first year or year and a half on the farm, so everything was done by hand. All the lights were oil lamps, and there were also gas lanterns in the house. You tried to use as much daylight as you could for chores because the rest of the time you had storm lanterns that could be taken outside for chores or used inside to illuminate the house.

The first days on the farm, we harvested with threshing machines, using binders to cut the grain. The grain was then put into stooks and collected using horses and a rack. The stooks were taken to the threshing machine which spit out the grain as if by magic, leaving the straw behind.

Harvest time was really exciting for a young person. The threshing crew might be five or six teams of horses with men loading the grain into the hay racks and taking it to the threshing machine to process. The horses had to be looked after, and the men had to be fed, so it was a big operation.

Threshing would start at about eight in the morning and finish at five or six at night. The regular chores still had to be done before and after the threshing. Because the horses and the men worked hard, it was a challenge to feed them all. You killed a lot of chickens, or whatever other animal was providing the meat, and you had to have lots of potatoes and vegetables. The fields were not too big, so the threshing team was usually only there for a day or two, but it was an event!

Growing a garden was a vital part of every farm, and we were pretty good at gardening. One year, we had an infestation of potato bugs in the garden. The solution was to pick the bugs off the plants and drop them in kerosene which would kill the bugs.

When we planted potatoes, we didn't get seed potatoes from the store like people do today. We just took old potatoes from our previous harvest that had eyes, and you would cut them up so that each piece had a few eyes. You would drop those or plant them three to a hill and then cover them up with the plow. We would have ten or fifteen rows that were each thirty feet long, and that resulted in a lot of potato plants. When we harvested, there were a lot of potatoes, and that was a major food source for us.

We also planted carrots, beets, turnips, and parsnips. I have no idea why we planted turnips since I'd never met anyone who liked them. But the garden was a big part of our sustenance from the vegetables we harvested, eating some right away, and preserving others for the winter.

The neighbours had a great crop of vegetable marrow one year which they shared with us. Phyl canned it and then made sandwiches with it for our school lunches. My recollection is that those sandwiches were so awful that we would try to auction them off at school. The hero of the day was the person who could exchange them for something that was a little better. Phyl took the blame for that, but she was just trying to feed us all and not waste. Our normal sandwich was baloney on slices of bread, and dessert was a sandwich with peanut butter and jam. I think I ate sandwiches for lunch for the first fifteen or twenty years of my life, and I still enjoy a good sandwich.

The road into our farm was like a little "s" that went around the old barn that was demolished, then passed the new barn and the chicken coop, curving around some granaries, and winding up to circle the house and go back out the other way. Winters were very hard on our roads which made it difficult to get around. With horses, it wasn't too bad, but once we got cars or trucks on the road, we often got stuck with the heavy snowfalls that were common during a Saskatchewan winter.

We didn't have indoor plumbing which meant no indoor toilet. There was a make-shift toilet in Mom and Dad's room consisting of a toilet seat on a five-gallon bucket that had to be emptied, but the rest of us had to go outside. I considered it a blessing to be a boy because you could urinate almost anywhere, while the girls had a bit more difficulty with that.

The yard around our house had bushes and trees on both sides which meant there were a lot of birds. I became interested in all these unique creatures that hadn't been part of our experience in southern Saskatchewan. We had orioles and wrens, woodpeckers, and blackbirds; almost every type of bird I could imagine. They were colourful and fascinated me with their songs and antics.

The barn swallows were something I had not seen before, and they were beautiful. They made their little houses out of mud underneath any eavestrough and could often be seen sitting on the telephone line that ran into our home. In later years, electricity provided more lines for them to sit on, and I never tired of watching their masterful flying.

I was an exceptional climber of trees and many of my adventures and discoveries happened several feet off the ground. Hawks always build their nests in the tallest poplar trees they can find, and I quickly became adept at shinnying up the fifteen feet or so until branches appeared to make the climb easier. For some reason, I thought raising hawks might be a worthwhile endeavour, so I climbed up to the nest, removed a couple of young hawks, and took them home. Turns out that hawks don't like bread soaked in milk, nor is it a healthy diet for them. After trying this a couple of times, I gave up the idea, and the hawk population was spared further interference.

Another nest that I wanted to explore up close was that of the great horned owl. There was a nest in a willow tree that I managed to climb where the young owls were almost ready to fly. As I poked my head over the edge of the nest, I saw the biggest yellow eyes I had ever seen. The little curved beak began to chatter and soon the mother owl came to the rescue. She was not very hospitable and demonstrated her displeasure as I quickly sought to extract myself from that willow tree. It was an unforgettable experience for sure!

I had no idea of how versatile ducks could be. One year, I found a couple of mallard ducks nesting in an old crow's nest. I'm not sure if they were anticipating a flood like back in Noah's time, but I did wonder how the young ducklings would get down from a nest that was fifteen feet above the ground. Perhaps their fluff would protect them when they were dropped from the nest, and they would go on to find the nearest body of water.

Springtime was always an exciting time. We waited to see who would discover the first crow to return, the first robin, and the first red-winged blackbird. Everyone wanted to win these contests and we kept our eyes and ears open. The other contest involved our favourite swimming holes. Because the well water had so many minerals that rendered it unsuitable for drinking or washing, every farm had a dugout that also served as a swimming hole. The competition was to see who would be the first person to go swimming in the spring.

One year, I surely won the competition since I walked across the snow still in the ditches, stripped off my clothes, and swam across the dugout as fast as I could. This was before cell phones with cameras, so you had to be able to tell the story and convince your buddies that you had been the first one in the swimming hole.

We only got to swim for about a month before the swimming holes were infested with a parasite that caused extreme itching, effectively bringing the swimming season to an end. Until that time, we swam in the dugout most school days.

Our favourite dugout was at the Spearing farm which was about a half-mile south of town. The dugout there was only about five feet deep, so we were not in danger of drowning. Our practice was to go behind the bush that was beside the dugout, strip off our clothes, and swim naked. I had heard stories about girls coming and stealing the clothes of nude swimmers, but that never happened to us. The other close swimming hole was east of town on the Warner farm.

I have a vivid memory of wanting to show my buddies how I could dive backwards. Standing on the edge of the dugout, I arched my back and prepared to do my famous backward dive. I didn't realize how shallow the dugout was and ended up burying my head in the mud at the bottom. I came up covered in muck, much to the hilarity of my audience.

Our yard had an abundance of little rabbits that I loved to watch. We got a mongrel dog that we named Soup because he was a mixture of several different breeds. Soup wasn't the smartest dog, but he sure enjoyed chasing those rabbits. It became a competition between him and the bunnies to see who would claim the yard as their territory. Soup finally won that challenge, and the rabbits kept to the bushes rather than hanging out in the yard.

Don in front on the left with Soup

We enjoyed the animals that were on our farm and became attached to them, but we understood that they were there to produce eggs, milk, and meat. We named them, but they were not pets. The dog was a bit different, but he also had a purpose. He was there to chase the cows when you wanted him to, and sometimes when you didn't want him to, but he was small enough that he wasn't really a challenge to the cows. They kind of ignored him or they ran at him, and he ran away and left them alone.

Our horses were very special to us; they were among the first animals we purchased when we moved to the farm. They were brown geldings with splashes of white on their legs. They weren't racehorses or draft horses, but they were what we would call "all-purpose" horses. We named them Hans and Prince. Hans was smaller and faster, and Prince, the bigger one, was my horse. They were used to do work on the farm such as plowing and hauling, but they were also used to get us to school. We lived four and a half miles from town, so it was about a thirty- to forty-five-minute trip for the horses to get us there. There was a barn at school to keep them in, and we would take along feed for them.

In addition to being our transport to school, the horses were used for pulling the stoneboat: a sort of sled or sledge which was used to haul things. They were also used to propel the small plough we used to plant our potatoes, and to pull the Fresno scoop that we used to dig the cellar under our first house on the farm.

When the horses weren't being used for farm work, they helped fuel my dreams of being a cowboy. Growing up, I read cowboy stories from the writer Zane Grey, and now I had the opportunity to practice being a cowboy myself! We didn't have saddles, so my brother and I would ride bareback. We weren't particularly good cowboys; without saddles we rode more like the Indians, but without their skill at staying on the horses.

Jerry riding Hans with a friend.

Jerry could stick to his horse like glue, but my pants were a little more slippery. When we were riding for pleasure, we would be galloping down the road when Jerry would turn into our driveway with his horse. My horse would turn in too, but I just kept travelling until I hit the ground. This necessitated finding something to help me crawl back up on the horse. I would grab its mane and shinny up its front leg.

Later, when I got to ride a horse with a saddle, I marvelled at how easy it was to stay on! I could hang onto the horn, put my feet in the stirrups, and found the saddle wasn't nearly as slippery as the horse's hide!

Muskrat hunting in the spring was a favourite pastime as well as an important source of income for me, and hunting on horseback was definitely a step up from hunting on foot. If I shot a muskrat while on the horse, I could retrieve the animal from the slough while staying nice and dry on top of my long-legged steed. The only trouble was that the horse didn't always like me shooting from its back.

On one occasion, Prince stepped sideways when I shot, and the sudden movement caused me to fall off. I got back on him and brought the barrel of my .22 down between his ears in anger. Thankfully his skull was very hard, and he wasn't injured, but the impact caused the stock of my gun to split. In later years, I used that .22 with a cracked stock as a visual aid when teaching in Christian boys' club to illustrate what a bad temper can do.

People often wonder why farm kids learn to hunt at such a young age. A lot of our hunting was to help control predators and pests, but we also hunted to supplement the family's meat supply. Our parents and experience taught us safety rules: you never carried a loaded gun when you were going to the hunting grounds; in theory, you should never carry a loaded gun at all. You never went through a fence holding your gun; you placed the gun on the ground facing away from you, and then you went through the barbed wire fence, picking up the gun once you were free of the fence. This helped to avoid accidents. The other safety rule was that you never walked ahead of someone who was carrying a loaded gun, since any accidental discharge could hit you.

There were still some memorable experiences and near-misses despite our training and better sense. I remember one time in particular when my buddies and I were harvesting crows. The crows were at the stage where they could jump out of the nest to be in the tree branches, but they couldn't quite fly yet. As usual, I was the person in the trees, given my love of climbing and lack of fear. There was a lot of activity and lots of crows and I remember hollering down: "Quit shooting! You're going to miss the birds and hit me!!"

My friends must have heeded my words since I'm still here to tell the story.

Another memorable experience was when Orvile and Edgar Dahl, Jack Ross, and I had finished an unsuccessful day of hunting. As we walked back across the field to the Dahl farm, carrying our .22 rifles and BB guns, we wondered what would happen if you shot a .22 shell with a BB. We laid a .22 bullet on the ground and shot at it with our BB guns.

We didn't have much luck hitting the shell from above, so we moved a little distance away for safety, lay on our stomachs, and shot at it. We would hear these little "pings," but didn't realize that we had hit the shell.

Finally, I moved a little closer to stand above the .22 shell, and I was successful in hitting it. We didn't take into account the fact that when a bullet is in the gun, it's held in place until the firing pin hits the back of the bullet, causing the powder to explode and the lead shell to go flying down the chamber and out the barrel of the gun. If we had remembered our physics lessons, we might have realized that when the shell has nothing to contain it, the gunpowder explosion will cause the heavier lead to fall out, while the lighter cartridge will go flying.

When I shot the BB and it hit the shell, the shell flew back and hit me just below the eye, cutting my flesh with the sharp edge. I wore that scar for a lot of years until the skin grew over and erased it. It was another experience where there could have been serious injury except for the hand of Providence.

One of my favourite hunting stories occurred after I had left Beatty to begin working in Yorkton. Jerry, who was the kindest and toughest brother anyone could have, let me borrow his car to go back to Beatty for a visit in the fall. The northern ducks had already gathered and were on their migration route. Edgar, Jack, and I had spotted an open water pond where the birds congregated, and we made plans to go hunting there.

Early the next morning before sunup, we gathered shotguns and two boxes of twenty-five shells each. As the sun rose, the noise of the thousands of mallards that were on the pond filled the air. We opened fire as the ducks came off the pond, and a number of ducks fell for the next hour as the birds circled and came back over the water. When we ran out of shells, we began to collect the ducks. I'm sure we only found about half the ducks that we had shot, but I vividly remember cleaning and plucking forty-seven mallards which then filled the Dahl's freezer. It was one of our most successful hunts.

5. School Days in Beatty

We went to school Monday through Friday, and I must say that our attendance record was probably 100 percent. We did not miss school because we were sick since we really didn't get sick, and it was more fun at school than it was at home. School was where you went to play games and see your friends. In our minds, school wasn't there for educating us but for socialization. We did get some education, but it was kind of incidental. Our friends were there, our social life was there, our sports life was there—why would we want to miss out on that?!

When we came to Beatty, I entered Grade 2 in the fall, and my lackadaisical performance in school made the teacher think I should go back to Grade 1. This was very traumatic for me. I'm not sure who intervened and what exactly happened, but I was finally allowed to continue on in Grade 2.

It was a time of new beginnings. It would be naïve to think that the changes occurring in Beatty were related to the arrival of the Smailes clan, but change was happening, and we jumped in with both feet. A new rink was to be constructed! The old rink was open-air and located close to the school grounds. Like most young boys, I was intrigued and somewhat foolish when it came to experimenting with frost on the goalposts. I learned that sticking a warm tongue on a frosty goalpost is not advisable no matter if the frost looks like ice cream. Food didn't taste the same for about a week after that experience, and part of my tongue may still be on those goalposts.

To raise funds for the new arena, an amateur hour was scheduled. I was always singing, and the teacher must have liked my voice. As a result, my classmate Ronnie Wingham and I were selected to sing at the amateur hour. Would you believe that we won first prize singing "Jimmy, Crack Corn and I Don't Care"? I still have the Melfort Journal announcement of it as proof!

What type of student was I? I believe that I have normal intelligence although there may be some who would debate that. Learning has never been beyond my capabilities, but often knowing why you are in school is a large part of the motivation to learn. I have always enjoyed humour and teasing, so it was definitely advantageous to be around people other than my siblings. I recall teasing Clifford Elliot, a fellow classmate, until he said in exasperation, "Don, too much is enough!!"

On another occasion, a group of us were discussing when we might get to have a school dance and I couldn't resist suggesting, "Let's have it on June 31st!"

"That's probably on a Sunday!" lamented my somewhat gullible classmate.

Beatty school picture. Don is on the right end of middle row, Pat is just behind him and to the right.

The school in Beatty had three rooms and each room had a teacher. Grades 1 through 4 were in one room, Grades 5 through 8 were in another, and high school was in the third room. As in many small-town schools, these classrooms were often used for other activities as well.

I must have been in Grade 5 or 6 when we were having a class photo taken out in front of the school. There were probably thirty to forty children there, and we were standing on the steps to facilitate getting everyone in the picture. Some of us kids were horsing around as kids are wont to do, and I got pushed from behind. I was on one of the top steps, and as I stumbled and began to fall, I was bashing the people in front of me. To avoid crushing one of the Haggland twins who was in Grade 1, I put my arms out to break my fall. I managed to avoid hurting the little first grader, but in the process, both of my wrists and arms were sprained. I went to the hospital in Melfort where an X-ray showed green fractures in both arms.

What do you do when you have casts on both arms and baseball season is beginning?!? My solution was to learn how to throw left-handed, since that arm wasn't quite as sore as my right one. With some practice, I became pretty good at throwing left-handed and got to be almost as accurate as when I threw with my right arm. Both of my wrists healed in time, and there was no lingering damage.

We would often play scrub which involved picking teams from the kids gathered and playing pretty much every position. We learned to pitch, to field grounders, to catch and throw. I may have been somewhat obsessed with the game and wanted to be Jackie Robinson. He was the best baseball player I knew. He was Black, or "coloured" as we would say at that time.

I didn't know anything about racial prejudice—I'm not sure I had even seen a person of colour in that part of Saskatchewan where we lived our sheltered lives. But I knew the best baseball player in the world was Jackie Robinson, and I wanted to be just like him.

My dad was ambidextrous and was equally skilled at hammering, sawing, and doing most things with either hand. I may have inherited some of that ability since I could bat left-handed as well as right-handed. Being a switch hitter was a lot of fun because I could confuse the pitcher by switching from right to left while up at bat. I had a little more power when batting right-handed and could hit line drives, pop flies, and home runs. However, batting left-handed positioned me closer to first base which is helpful when you're not the fastest runner. I could hit the ball down the third base line and get off to first right away, usually beating the throw to first base. That was a favourite strategy of mine.

In later years, when I went to Bible school in Chattanooga, Tennessee, I was on the baseball team as catcher. I'd never caught for baseball before, since we played fastball or softball, but I managed to catch whatever the pitchers threw. I also got pretty good at throwing to the bases when a runner was trying to steal. One game that we played, I hit a line drive over third base while batting left-handed, knocking in the only run that we got. I think we lost that game 25–1, but I was responsible for getting that one runner home.

As a catcher, you see a lot of foul balls, and some of these caused me to see stars. If a pitcher is throwing curve balls, the batter will connect and BAM! The ball goes way higher than a normal hit into the outfield. I would try to catch the ball before it hit the ground but would get so dizzy running after the ball while looking way up and trying to judge where it would come down that I often fell down without catching it.

Beatty School Boys' Ball Team. Jerry is in the back row on the left. Don is second from the right in front with his catcher's mitt.

I probably could have been a better player, but we really had no coaches. Add to that the fact that in springtime before softball season begins, you have snowball season. As an avid snowballer, I would have pretty much thrown my arm out during the many snowball fights we had before I could pick up a baseball.

We would also play soccer and occasionally competed against other schools. I remember one game we played against the team from Weldon. They had a pretty big guy on defence, and in the process of trying to get past him, my shoulder hit his face. Upon examining my painful shoulder, I discovered a tooth mark that had gone right through my shirt! He ended up with a broken tooth which was arguably worse, but I became the hero of my team. I can't remember whether we won or not, but I sure did enjoy my hero status.

It's amazing how sports became a source of identity. I was at least average or above average in sports. When we picked teams, I was always chosen and was usually picked first or second. That gave me status with the other kids, which helped with my self-esteem.

Going back to academics, I never failed a course. In fact, through the years in school, I was always recommended to go on to the next grade. We often wrote departmental exams and I managed to do well on those. While I may not have been above average in intelligence, I could generally figure out the right answer on multiple choice tests by logic and elimination based on what I did know. In our graduating class of Grade 12, there were eight students and only two passed all the subjects. I was one of those two.

Beatty High School Class. Don is second from the right in the back

Lest you think I was too good to be true, I did get into trouble at school on a few occasions. While in Grade 7 or 8, John Middleton and I were fooling around in the hall, and we managed to break a large window in the school. Of course, we were responsible to replace it, and I was so grateful that the Middletons were in a better economic position than our family, since there was no way we could have afforded to replace such a big window.

We often did foolish things when we were playing softball as well. I was probably in high school, but for some reason, we were playing a game that involved all the young people from Grade 1 and up. One of the players was a small boy in first grade who wore glasses. He came up to bat, and I was catching, but instead of using a catcher's mitt, I was "catching" with another bat. This little guy swung at the pitch and missed, spinning all the way around due to the energy he put into that swing. Unfortunately, I didn't miss and hit the ball right into his face, breaking his glasses which then cut his face. I felt horrible.

The incident was totally my fault and I had to take this boy in to his dad, who was the first-grade teacher, and confess what I had done. Fortunately, this student and his dad were incredibly gracious, and I didn't get into the trouble I should have. It was one of those occasions where you learn from doing something foolish that you should never do it again.

Halloween was an interesting time. We farm kids would come to town and go around getting some treats because we didn't get many treats at home. We played a few tricks too and made some mischief. One Halloween, we got into the small one-room high school building that also served as a concession during sports or field days. The windows were all on one side of the building, and some of us went in through those windows, armed with screws and screwdrivers. We put all the desks in front of the door and screwed them down into the floor so that it was impossible to open the door because of the desks. We then made our escape out the window.

Another year, we put desks up the flagpole. Somehow, we managed to attach them to the rope that raised the flag so that before the flag could be raised the next morning, the desks had to be taken down.

A subsequent year, we cut a foot out of the clothesline at a few places in town. When you cut a foot out of the clothesline, you either have to move the end poles closer together or splice the clothesline to make it reach. This makes it hard to roll out and back when you want to hang the laundry. It wasn't really destructive mischief, but about a year after we did that, I remember walking down the street in Beatty and being confronted by one of the victims of our prank who said, "You are the person who cut our clothesline!"

I'm sure my face turned ash white, and he knew he had found the guilty party. He didn't have me arrested or beat me up, but he probably should have thumped me.

Every school had Christmas concerts, and our school was no exception. It was fun being part of the program. Teachers would have us practise plays, and I was usually in the production which I enjoyed very much. Sometimes, they would have music and what they called "marches" where we would march to a song and interact with one another. Somehow, I never got into that, but I remember participating in comedy skits and was very comfortable being a clown.

When I have returned to Beatty and seen the town hall as an adult, I don't understand how we could perform in such a small building, but we did. We had amateur hours there that were occasionally carried on the radio in Prince Albert to raise money for different causes, and it was a lot of fun to participate in those too. Our small town had tremendous community spirit.

When we came to Beatty, it was a thriving little rural community. There were five elevators: two Searles, one Pool, one Home, and one National which gave the farmers a choice of where they took their grain. If you had a two-ton truck, that was a big truck. Much of the grain was delivered in the early days with horses and wagons, so the elevators seemed big in our minds, although they were small compared to the buildings today. From the elevator, the grain was moved by rail to the marketplace.

The farms were mostly half-section farms. If you had a quarter-section, it likely wasn't adequate to make a living, but if you had more than a half-section, you were a big operation. All the farms were run by families who raised lots of kids in addition to the other crops.

Our family had four kids going to school; in later years, if everyone was home, we were five, but some were not in school anymore. Most families had three or four kids, so every half-mile to mile, there was a farm with some youngsters. All those families made up our small community, and we had a lot of fun with so many kids around.

In Beatty, in addition to the five elevators, there were two general stores where you got your groceries. There was a hardware store that sold everything from coal to lumber and anything you needed for building and running a farm. There were two churches: a United church and a Gospel Assembly church, with an Anglican church being built in later years. Rounding out the community was a curling rink and a skating rink across from the town hall.

A major activity in rural Saskatchewan was the 4-H beef club. My brother and I and probably both Phyllis and Pat were involved in this at different times, raising calves and then selling them at auction. Raising an animal was a wonderful learning experience, and 4-H was a great educational and developmental organization. We learned how to keep records since you had to keep track of everything that you fed your calf, and we learned how to care for the animals.

We didn't have the best breeds of cattle, but we always had a calf. Both Jerry and I won awards for our ability to judge cattle, and Jerry won the highest award in all of Saskatchewan for his ability to judge. He won more than one wristwatch, which was a much-coveted prize, and at one time he won the equivalent of a trip to the Toronto Royal

Winter Fair by being the top judge in Saskatchewan. His partner in the competition didn't do as well as he did, so he didn't get to go to Toronto, but he had the highest score on record. It's no accident that he later made his living as a cattleman.

Jerry and Phyl with their 4-H calves

I got my name on a few trophies there for general achievement; I was the secretary of the beef club one year and kept good records. It was a wonderful place to learn how to speak in public, and between 4-H and church, I really learned how to express myself in front of an audience.

Our leaders in the 4-H club were our neighbours, and they had good cattle. They were wonderful people both as teachers and as examples of upstanding members of the community. At the end of the season, we had an achievement day where we would show our cattle and get prizes in different categories. There were prizes for showmanship, the best meat cattle, and judging. We never won prizes for optimal meat quality for our animals, but we were good at judging cattle.

Roy Anderson was our 4-H leader, and I recall a time when my best friend Jack Ross and I went to his place to milk his cows for him. The Andersons had a hired man, so I'm not sure why we thought we needed to help with the milking on this occasion, but we gathered the cows into the barn and started the process.

Not all cows were as cooperative as our Bessie, and they would let you know they were displeased by flicking a manure coated tail at your face or stepping into the milk bucket and tipping it over. I had one of the Anderson's cows in the milking pen, with the milk pail between my knees to prevent it being kicked over, and settled onto the milking stool. That cow kicked me halfway across the barn, not once but three or four times. If ever there was an instance of animal cruelty, this was it! I lost my temper and grabbed a nearby pitchfork to defend myself. I think we eventually gave up and let the cattle back out into the yard. Just goes to show that no good deed goes unpunished!

The other fun activity we did as kids was to go to farm boys camp when the fair came to Melfort. There again, we had contests, learning to identify weeds and plants from the area. Jerry had a book with pictures of different weeds, and I was able to remember the names of the various plants from looking at this book. This netted me third prize in the district for weed identification.

Fairs were also a wonderful place for entertainment, especially the midway with all the exciting rides. There were performances and horse races that were fun to watch. The challenge I faced was that I was always bothered by motion sickness, even in the car. If I was in the back of a truck where there was air flow, I was fine, but any time I was in an enclosed vehicle or on a ride that spun around, my stomach rebelled.

That didn't discourage me in the least from going on rides when the fair came to town. My friends didn't want to be anywhere near me when I did this, because my ruddy complexion would take on a greenish tinge and I would lose whatever was in my stomach in very short order. In later years when I learned to drive myself, motion sickness was no longer a problem except perhaps for my passengers. However, I do try to stay away from midway rides for everyone's sake!

Sometimes we were able to take the horses to town in the evening for a hockey game. We had a "caboose" which was a small shelter about six feet by eight feet that could be put on top of the stoneboat. This little structure had benches along the sides and a window at the front that allowed the passengers to see and speak to the horses. There were even small holes in the front for the reins to go through so no one had to get their hands cold. In the front left corner of the caboose was a small stove with a four-inch chimney that allowed you to build a little fire and keep everyone warm.

After the game, we would get in the caboose, tie the reins to the horses, and start them on the way home with a "Get up!" We would then curl up around the little stove in the caboose and sleep. Some forty-five minutes later, the horses would stop and we would wake up at our farm which was four and a half miles from where we started. Those horses had no trouble finding their way home.

Jerry in the caboose. Beatty, 1951

In the winter when we would take the caboose to school, we had to be careful to shut the door when we parked it for the day. For some reason, if the door was left open, any dogs roaming wild would go in and pee on the stove. This resulted in unpleasant fragrances when the stove was later lit for warmth!

When the horses were no longer needed on the farm for work, they were sold, and it fell to me to take them to town. I will never forget that trip to Melfort, riding my horse, Prince, while leading Hans. It was the longest and shortest fifteen-mile ride of my life, and I shed more than a few tears saying good-bye to these faithful animals. From Melfort, they were shipped off to become fertilizer or fox food, and that was the end of my journey with horses.

6. Tsunami of 1947

While I was becoming oriented to school and having all these new experiences, there were other things happening in our family that we kids didn't notice. Mom and Dad had been reunited after five or six years of separation due to the war and our relocation to Beatty. They were still very much in love and the expression of that love once again resulted in pregnancy. As an eight-year-old, I wasn't very observant and really didn't know much about babies and pregnancy. I was blissfully ignorant of any changes in our family, being much occupied with exploring all the other things that fill a young boy's imagination. In any case, my first clue that Mother was with child was when her labour pains began on June 16th. She was taken to the Melfort Hospital, probably with the tractor. After several hours of labour, a new life entered the world late in the evening of June 16th. We were told that our family had a brand-new member. She was named Evelyn but became "Lynn" for short.

Apparently, Mom's birthing experience was the third or fourth birth that day and evening in Melfort Hospital. She was hemorrhaging, and there was no blood supply, so in the early hours of June 17th, Mother left this earth. This was totally unexpected. What does a young boy know about birth? Nothing. What does a young boy of eight know about death? Even less. What does a young boy who enjoyed being the youngest and basking in the centre of his mother's attention know about suddenly not having a mother? Her death caused a tsunami in my young life and in our family. Our whole world was upset as we were left without the person who had been the heart and anchor of our home.

Our maintenance and support as a family became Aunt Lois and Uncle Clifford. Clifford was my mom's younger brother, and they lived in the Melfort area. Apparently, Dad went to their place to deliver the news, and it was there that my cousin Harold remembers him crying and weeping disconsolately. Dad, to my knowledge, had no spiritual connection prior to this. My cousin Harold remembers a long period of time that Dad spent on his knees before God, asking for help.

What do you do when your world has suddenly been destroyed?

What must it have been like to have gone through five years of separation during the war, and then finally starting a new life together, only to have your wife and sweetheart snatched away, leaving you with five children, including a new baby? To add insult to injury, Dad regularly donated blood to treat an iron surplus in his own body. How awful to have your wife perish from lack of something you yourself have too much of!

The change in my life was immediate, though this changed all our lives. What do you do with a new baby when there is no mother to care for her? A plan was made the next day to send Baby Lynn to one of our cousins, Wilma (we knew her as Chubb). She took the baby for a short time, but it soon became apparent that Chubb's life was not very solid. Unbeknownst to all of us, she was dealing with substance abuse and was perhaps a closet alcoholic.

When word of the unsuitability of this situation came to light, Lynn was sent to my Aunt Elsie and Uncle Sid where she spent a year or so. Uncle Sid was Dad's younger brother. Again, this was not an ideal situation despite it being a loving and stable home. Aunt Elsie was expecting a child of her own and at about the same time as Lynn's arrival, she gave birth to her daughter. Again, Lynn was moved; this time to one of our Shaunavon neighbours, Grace Harden, who cared for her.

Phyl (on right) bringing Lynn home from Grace Harden in Shaunavon.

As the summer of that year progressed, more changes occurred in our home. Phyllis, who was finishing Grade 10, quit school and took over the responsibility of being the woman of the house. It was a daunting challenge, and she did it amazingly well. She became the cook and managed the household in such a way that within a year, when Lynn was only a year old, we brought her back home. Phyllis sacrificed her schooling to take on that role, and while we may not have fully appreciated her sacrifice at that time, she certainly made a huge difference in our family. Looking back, I wonder: How can someone in tenth grade take on all the responsibilities of mothering and caring for a young one while doing all the chores that an active farm requires? She was certainly stretched beyond what anyone could imagine.

Dad was really no help during this time as his life totally fell apart. He was often absent, and when he was at home, his dissolute habits meant that home was no longer a safe place, particularly for his daughters. Our home became a place where each person was just trying to survive.

I reverted to wetting the bed and even wetting my pants at school. It wasn't that I was too lazy to get up and go to the bathroom; I was just unaware of the urge to urinate until I woke up in a wet, smelly bed. There was probably some teasing and definitely a lot of shame in this, particularly when I wet my pants at school. I'm thankful that I don't remember a lot about this period, and I'm sure God has done a lot of healing to enable me not to be affected by the trauma of this time in my young life.

I do remember after Mom's death that the horses were a source of comfort to me. I would go into the barn and get onto the back of one of the horses standing in the stall. I often mounted facing backwards and would lie down with my cheek pressed to the warmth of the animal's rump. In the dim light with the quiet animal sounds and smells, I would often fall asleep and escape the pain of loss for a few hours at least.

When the horses were in the pasture, the best way to catch them was to get a pail of mush. When they came to get the oats, you could put a halter or bridle on them as they ate. One afternoon after Mom had died, I was in the pasture trying to bring the horses in. I had the pail of oats, but as I tried to slip the halter over the horse's head, he ran away. In my frustration, I swore at him. Almost immediately, I was struck by the conviction that my mother would not have wanted me to swear. I dissolved into tears and fell to the ground weeping. It was probably my first episode of truly mourning the loss of my mother.

God, in His providence and goodness, provided wonderful families and caring women who did the best they could to help us during this time. We experienced Jesus living in and through these loving women and families who nurtured and cared for us. Mrs. Vivian Chute was one of these ladies. She had two children: Alice, who was about the same age as my sister Phyllis, and Earl, who was between Gerald and me in age. Mrs. Chute became a substitute mom for us, caring for us almost as her own.

I remember our first Christmas without Mom. We were invited to the Chute home, and we received presents from their family. My friends persuaded me that the nighttime stars would look really bright if I looked at them from the bottom of a coat sleeve. I gamely put my face into the arm of a coat to look up the sleeve. The sleeve sure did make for a dark place, but the stars that I saw were rather wet as my mischief-making friends poured water down the sleeve and into my face. It's good to have a little fun in the midst of life's storms.

7. Beatty and Family Changes

Beatty is a special place for me. I have so many wonderful memories of amazing people there, as well as the many fun and challenging adventures we experienced together. This is where eternal friendships were formed. The Beatty cemetery is a precious place. Every time I am in the area, the first place I go is to my mother's grave site where I have a memorial service. I thank God for the mother that He used not only to bring me into the world but also to lead me to my spiritual rebirth. I'll sing a hymn and have a time of prayer, thanking God for this place and remembering His goodness to me. The Bible says that we look forward to a time when our mortal bodies will be reunited with our spirits that have passed on at death. Until that time, cemeteries and burial places are sacred places of contemplation and thanksgiving as we reflect on the lives that have formed us.

Don at Mudge's grave, 2020

Following Mom's death, there were other changes in the dynamics of our family. When Phyllis quit school in Grade 10 to take over managing the household, Gerald would have been in eighth grade, Pat in sixth grade, and I would have been entering Grade 4.

Gerald became a man immediately. He began working on other farms to help with the family finances. He continued to go to school in Beatty, finishing his Grade 10 there. Then he went to Carley, near Nipawin, and the Bible school there, where he finished his Grade 11 and 12. During this time, he worked for the Ekstrands and also for the Evans as a hired man. He may even have lived at their place while working, since he wasn't at home all the time during this period. Pat and I continued at home with Phyl and Lynn who was growing up as a little girl.

Dad's life became that of an absentee father—whether being at the farm without Mom there was too painful a reminder of his loss, I don't know, but he was seldom at home. Prior to this, he had been a hard worker and had even done farm work for other people in addition to managing his own farm.

The loss of his life partner, however, had reduced him to a shadow of his former self, and he fell into a pattern of drinking and running up debts. My sister Pat recalls that Mom had always managed the family purse since Dad wasn't good with money. He would borrow, then fabricate stories and outright lies, leaving behind a trail of outstanding bills.

When he wasn't at home, he was usually in Prince Albert where he had begun to frequent the Legion. Perhaps he was searching for friends to help make sense of his situation, and certainly he was using more alcohol than was good for him. In any case, he was not running the farm, and as a result, the farm debts increased faster than we could work them off.

During this period, Dad met Lorna Taylor in Prince Albert. As they began to spend time together, she became pregnant. In June of 1950, they were married, and a second family was on the way.

By this time, Phyllis went off to Tisdale to begin a nursing program. She lived in residence there and became a licensed practical nurse. Her first assignment was in Wadena, Saskatchewan. While there, she enrolled as an adult in high school to finish her Grade 12. Afterwards, she took on the responsibility of raising Lynn. Pat also left home to finish her schooling and to become a nurse, following in her sister's footsteps. As a result, I ended up at home alone, and have very few memories of that time. Perhaps it is a mercy that I can't recall much of what was certainly a difficult time as I finished Grade 12 in Beatty.

The combining of two families was very traumatic. Lorna had never experienced living in conditions like ours which were rough to begin with being out in the country, but certainly became worse as the farm and house fell into disrepair. There was a new baby arriving every year or two, beginning with Laurie in the fall of 1950, then Gail, then Carol and Graham, and she was having to manage all this with little support from her husband.

At that time, Dad was still officially on the farm, but between the needs of the new children and the struggles of the first family, there was significant turmoil and conflict in the home. I was a mouthy kid and had no trouble speaking my mind in family discussions or arguments. I remember on at least one occasion having a cup bounced off my head by a frustrated stepmother who was in a situation that was totally incompatible with raising young children.

We were all in survival mode, and it was not a fun time for anyone. Dad was away from the farm or in Prince Albert much of the time. He was drinking more, and the farm was not being run well at all. I was still going to school but spent as much time as I could at the neighbours.

During this time, Lorna brought her niece, who was probably a little older than I was, into our home to help with the farm chores and babies. This girl was probably in about tenth grade and was assigned sleeping quarters on the "female side" of the partition upstairs.

One day, I was out crushing grain for the livestock and found two or three frozen mice in the barn. They were adult mice that hadn't survived the winter, and I decided to play a trick on this attractive young lady who had joined our household. I placed the mice in her bed during the daytime when she was helping with other chores and waited for her reaction at bedtime.

Three days passed with no evidence that my "surprise" had been found. I suggested to her that she should make her bed. When she did, she discovered the mice, and I found myself running barefoot in the snow from the house to the barn, being chased by a young lady with a broom who wasn't as amused by my prank as I had been!

The Dahl family were our closest neighbours, and they were truly

God's gift to me during this time. Clifford Dahl and his wife Olive had seven children ranging in age from Orvile who was a bit younger than me to Florence who was already away from home and married. They were wonderful neighbours, and I probably spent at least as much time at their house as I spent at my own.

Mr. Dahl became like a father to me. While he was a man who had only a fourth-grade education, he had taught himself to read and had been a grain buyer. He was an exceptional carpenter and a hard worker. He was a man of few words but great wisdom. He and his wife accepted me like a son and taught me how to work.

I was often at their place for milking time and got plenty of experience as they had about twenty cows. I was there for building projects and was often at their table for meals. Because we went to school together, and because of the number of children in the Dahl family, we played games together in the evening.

The Dahls had a big barn and they had lots of sparrows—so many that they became a nuisance. In order to control the population of these feathered pests, we would capture them at night. We would get up in the loft where the sparrows rested on the support beams that ran across the rafters. Being the climber that I was, I would get up on those rafters and could easily move across from beam to rafter, catching the birds in my hand, wringing their necks, and throwing them down for the cats. That was our solution to pest control.

There was seldom a thought to safety, and I often wonder how we never fell off those rafters. At ten feet above the barn floor, a fall might have knocked some sense into my head, but then again, I was a pretty tough and stubborn kid who didn't think too long about consequences or danger.

The Dahls had a team of horses called "Buster" and "Jenny." Buster, the gelding, was a big draft horse and very powerful. When you went into the barn and slid the door open, the electrical light switch was right above Buster's rump. These horses were gentle and wouldn't cause any trouble if you talked to them. But if you didn't talk to them, they didn't know who you were and would react in unexpected ways.

I remember coming into the barn one night and, rather than talking to the horses to let them know who I was, I just reached for the light switch. WHAM! Buster's hoof grazed my chin, bloodied my lips and nose, and sent my hat flying ten or fifteen feet across the barn. Two inches further up and that hoof would've caught me right under the chin and I would've probably followed Mother to heaven.

God's providence in sustaining our lives is a mystery. If it's true that we have guardian angels, I may have worn out more than my fair share since there have been a few near-death experiences where I was blissfully unaware of the danger.

I have great gratitude to the Dahls and still consider them dear friends. They were truly among God's special agents for good in my life. I remember one time in particular coming home from school in the dead of winter when there were still quite a few of our family at home. We couldn't get the stove going, and the house was freezing!! We ended up going over to the Dahls where we spent the night. The next morning, Dad returned to the house and was able to get the fires burning again so we could go home.

Our neighbours were aware of the trouble that we were having as a family. They didn't intervene by calling the police or social services—that just wasn't done, and there certainly weren't the social programs that now exist to help families and children. Our neighbours simply gathered around us and were always there to help with whatever we needed.

Our next closest neighbours were the Andersons. Roy, our 4-H beef club leader, and his wife Vi were wonderful neighbours. Roy met an untimely death, suffering a heart attack in his forties, but they were very good friends for my dad and my stepmother. Dad and Lorna spent many hours playing cards and visiting together as couples during the time all the children were being born.

Another indelible memory during that time was when Laurie was just a baby. She was sick with some kind of upper airway respiratory problems and was crying in obvious distress as she fought to breathe. I remember getting down on my knees and praying that God would intervene and spare her life. Those were hard times, but God was with us, and Laurie recovered.

Other neighbours who were instrumental in our lives were Algot Erickson and his family. Their land was right across from our half-quarter. I knew that quarter of their land very well because it had a lot of bush, and I knew where every crow's nest was in the area. We didn't have as much community with them, since they were in the municipality off Kinistano, and we were in Flett Springs, but after I had left the farm and it was being sold, they became good friends. My brother Brent, from the second family, has wonderful memories of being at their place and being taken to a Gospel meeting. God touched him and helped him heal from a congenital hip deformity that had affected him since birth.

Our church affiliation was primarily with the Gospel Assembly Church and it was a good church. The gospel was preached every Sunday, and Sunday school with Mrs. Hattie Lees was instrumental in my religious formation. Church became an important social outlet too, as many of our friends went to the Gospel Assembly and Baptist church even though we attended different schools. The church and 4-H club provided us with great friendships.

While in Grade 11 or early Grade 12, my dad was already absent from the farm most of the time. The second family had moved back to Prince Albert, and Dad was working there. One day, he was up on a ladder washing windows when a piece of the ladder moved. Down he fell, some thirty-four feet, hitting his head on several rungs on the way down. An elderly gentleman tried to catch him and probably saved his life.

I heard the news in Beatty, and Stan Maxwell, a family friend, gave me a ride to Saskatoon where Dad had been taken to the university hospital. When I came into Dad's hospital room, he was swathed in bandages, and his whole body seemed to be crooked. As he looked at me, his torso appeared twisted at a ninety-degree angle away from his head. He was badly bashed up, and the sight of his injuries made me woozy.

A nurse came in, took one look at me, and instructed, "Sit down and put your head between your legs before you faint!"

I had a flashback to the only other time I had been in hospital at age six having my tonsils removed. The smells of ether and antiseptic triggered that feeling of falling into the dark tunnel of anaesthesia—not a pleasant recollection!

My dad eventually recovered from that fall; he was a pretty tough character and had survived many incidents that could've been fatal. However, he continued to struggle with alcohol and debt. Perhaps the combined experiences of fighting in a war, losing a beloved wife, and never being able to keep up with life and the growing needs of his family were too much for him to face.

I returned to the farm in Beatty where I managed to finish school. Those last couple of years were very difficult and lonely as I was the only remaining member of the family still on the farm.

Don on left dressed for high school grad

The farm had fallen into disrepair, and there was no money for proper feed. I have a poignant memory of a beautiful six-month-old calf dying of malnutrition. There was really nothing I could do but pull the carcass into the manure pile. Dad owed money to almost everyone in the area, and it was impossible to rescue the farm. Eventually the homestead was sold, the debts consolidated, and the Beatty chapter of my life finished.

8. Yorkton, 1956

When I graduated from Grade 12 in June of 1956, my brother Gerald was the assistant manager of the livestock pool in Yorkton, Saskatchewan. There was an opening for a yard man, and I accepted that position. The day after leaving school, I was on the road to Yorkton and my new adventure.

In the early 1950s, farm kids didn't bother with an official driving licence, but driving in the big city was another thing entirely! I needed a licence! When I moved to Yorkton, I was eighteen and borrowed Jerry's car to take my driving test. The RCMP officer who was administering the test got into the car with me, and we began. I went through a stop sign, and he instructed me to take him back to the barracks; I had failed the test.

On my second attempt, I took the officer to pick up his uniform at the dry cleaners. I successfully passed the test and his only comment was: "You need to slow down when you go through school zones."

Jerry and I rented a room from the Grothoffs in Yorkton. Tom and Elsie Grothoff were of German heritage and were wonderful folks who lived in a large house about a mile north of Yorkton on York Road. They charged us thirty dollars a month which included all meals, packed lunches, a bed, laundry, and whatever they could do for us. In exchange, we did most of the farm chores for Tom.

Tom was a good farmer, and he owned about a half-section of land. He also rented land from the Yorkton airport that had previously been used to train pilots during the war. There were a few buildings remaining on the land that had been residences for the trainees, but most of it was field and we farmed it. It was an amazing sight to be out there at night on a tractor doing farm work when a DC-3 would come in for a landing at the airport. I had never seen the lights of an airplane as it was landing before, but it lit up the whole field.

That field was also the scene of some drama one fall when someone—probably Tom—decided to burn some stubble after harvest. The wind came up, and the fire quickly got out of control, almost burning up the neighbour's field. We were all trying to beat out the fire and get it back under control. Somehow, with God's help, disaster was averted, and we managed to put the fire out.

Tom's main job was to buy and transport animals in his little truck for the Propp Meat Market, later called Mid- West Packers, which was located right next to the stockyards. Tom was a big man with grey hair cut in a brush cut. He had an enormous scar on his head just above his right ear. This was the result of being run over by a lumber wagon or farm wagon when he was a child in Germany.

Whatever scars he had on the outside, on the inside he had one of the largest and most generous hearts I've ever experienced. Much like my older brother, Tom was a father figure to me. He was a man of integrity, and while not religious, he was a genuine Christian man. He attended church but was not involved in the activities and committees. His was a quieter faith of actions rather than words. One Christmas, Jerry and I got him a Bible in his native German which became a prized possession.

Tom's farm included a barn and Tom often had some cattle that he was feeding and preparing for market. I don't recall there being calves, but we always had some livestock. While working at the stockyard, I was able to buy a young heifer from the yard and join the 4-H beef club. I enjoyed being active in that and ended up winning the showmanship award for my yearling. The Propp Food Market bought my calf at a premium price, and Jerry said, "They overpaid for that, and you owe them a big thank you!" I was more than happy to pay that debt of gratitude.

Don with 4-H cow in Yorkton

Work at the stockyards was dirty and smelly, but what can you expect when you're dealing with animals and manure? My job was to help manage and move the cattle brought in by the farmers for sale. At sale time, I was responsible for penning the cattle as they came off the scale, then putting them in the new pens for the owners who had bought them. I would be running the whole day at full speed, and, not to brag, but when I left that job, they replaced me with two people. I was fit, enjoyed the challenge of the job, and felt valued and respected.

It's difficult to describe the barely controlled chaos that was a livestock sale. The calves had to be penned as they arrived, and sometimes there were lambs as well in the spring that were penned along with the calves. When the sale was on, a calf would be brought to the sales ring, and when the new owner of the calf was announced, the calf would be taken to the scale for weighing, then I would run to take the animal to the new owner's pen.

Things got really exciting when there were both lambs and calves in an enclosure. More than once, when you opened the gate, your chest would feel the impact of the lambs' hooves as they charged and sent you reeling back. You would land on your backside as the escapees scooted down the alley. There wasn't any place for them to go, so you either laughed or swore, picked yourself up, and went to corral them back into the appropriate pen.

There were many other activities at the stockyard, but the highlight was at the end of the day when all the animals that had been purchased were loaded up to be shipped to Winnipeg. The big transport trucks would arrive and back into the loading docks where the animals would be brought from the pens to be loaded up for their journey to market. The truckers had to be very precise in backing up to the loading dock so that there was no gap between the back of the truck and the dock. When the cattle were being loaded into the back of the truck, you couldn't afford for a leg to go through the gap and result in a break. The trick was to get the cattle running and to be right behind them so that you could close the partition behind them. If you didn't get the partition closed, the animal turned around and then you'd be the one running as they chased you back into the pen. That was when you found out how quickly you could climb a fence, particularly if there were some big bulls behind you! This was our version of a rodeo, and it was a lot of fun. We would normally load anywhere from three to five trucks a night, and they were off to Winnipeg. Then, you closed up the yard, fed the remaining cattle, and went home.

We also loaded boxcars that were then shipped by rail, some of them to Eastern Canada. Those were different loading experiences, since they usually consisted of small animals, or feeder cattle as we would call them. These would go to Ontario where they were fattened up for market.

Saturdays were the days we cleaned up the stockyards. We had to clean up all the pens, removing the manure and preparing for the activities of the coming week. Our foreman, Gord, was a wonderful man. He was patient with us young guys, making sure we worked hard, but also letting us know we were appreciated. I enjoyed the status of having a bigger brother who was highly respected, not only because of his position, but because of his talent and work ethic.

Jerry was excellent at his job and so was highly valued in the stockyards. He would usually only be in a position for about a year before he was promoted to another role where he would get even more experience. As the assistant manager to Bert Berwick, our manager, he was making decisions on buying cattle for resale to others. Many of the people in the sales ring worked for Swift's, Canada Packers, Burns, or some of the other meat-packing plants. Others were buyers who would purchase the cattle and then resell them at a profit. All were wonderful people who enriched that chapter of my life.

During slower times when we were not buying or selling cattle, I was introduced to a new card game. As an evangelical Christian, I had never been allowed to play cards since they were believed to be evil. But in the stockyards, they played a game called "Smear" or "High Low Jack" where you had to bid on how good you thought your cards were. I watched the others play, and it wasn't long before I got the hang of the game and was invited to participate.

Our auctioneer was without question the best gambler. Charlie would often go to Las Vegas on his holidays to gamble, and he had a talent for it. If he was addicted to it, it was because he was good at it and always made money. His gambling didn't have a detrimental effect on his family since he always had money in his "smear" or gambling account. He was quite a character and a great guy.

All of the people in the business treated me with great respect. It was a good time of learning how to work hard, and I found that I loved to work. I never missed a day, and there was no such thing as overtime; you worked until the job was done. You got to work early, did your job, and looked for things you could do to learn more. I spent fifteen months there, working for the Saskatchewan Wheat Pool livestock division in Yorkton, and they were good months.

Jerry, in addition to being a hard worker, good substitute father, and great big brother, was also quite attractive. He was built like famed Canadian hockey player Bobby Hull, very muscular, and he had a great smile. His dark wavy hair, probably inherited from Mom who had very wavy hair, was so tightly curled in places, people wondered if there was some African American in his background. Jerry was never without a girlfriend—such a handsome, hardworking, charming guy was bound to be popular with the ladies.

We both attended the German Baptist church in Yorkton. The Sunday morning service was in German and neither of us understood the language. I spent my time during the service looking at the girls and reading my Bible. There may have been a connection between the number of pretty, young German girls and our attendance at the church. Jerry's girlfriend at the time had a best friend who was the most beautiful girl I had ever met. She was only fifteen, but I was smitten.

9. Romance

I found out that this lovely blonde girl's name was Geraldine Ziolkowski. What a mouthful! I had no idea how to spell either "Geraldine" or "Ziolkowski," but her nickname was "Deany" and I could remember that. There was a picnic at York Lake on July 1st, and I was introduced to Deany and some others as the new boy in town. I wanted to make an impression on this beautiful girl with the wavy blonde hair, so I said, "You may not believe this, but I can remove a hair from your head without you ever feeling it."

She was skeptical, so I had to demonstrate. I took a strand of her hair between my fingers, and just before pulling it out, I banged her on the head with my other fist. She was so surprised at being hit on the head by this crazy boy that she didn't feel the hair being pulled out. After making a first impression like that, it was a wonder she ever agreed to see me again!

I didn't know how to spell "Ziolkowski," but to my uneducated ears, it sounded like it would begin with an "S." I looked all through the "S-es" in the Yorkton phone book in vain before asking my landlord and landlady for help. They patiently explained that "Ziolkowski" was with a "Z."

I was a shy kid, but I really liked this girl, so I found her phone number and called her.

"Hello, Deany? This is Don. Would you go to a stock car race with me this weekend?"

After mustering my courage to ask her on a date, I got a flat-out refusal. Apparently, she had been dating another Don at the time and didn't want to go out with him anymore. When I called, she thought I was him and politely but firmly refused me. I was crushed. Thankfully I was also persistent and didn't give up. We were able to sort out which Don was which, and she agreed to go on a date with me.

Deany in the garden with her mother looking on from the porch

One of our first dates was to see a football game in Regina with my brother and his girlfriend. That was a memorable trip! I was in love with this girl. She was unlike anyone I had ever met.

Driving to Regina, we listened to the Yankees playing the Dodgers in the World Series on the radio. It was an unforgettable game, made even more enjoyable since my brother Jerry was a Yankee fan while I was a Dodger fan. Nothing like a bit of friendly fan rivalry to liven up a drive! In this game, the Yankee pitcher, Don Larsen, pitched a perfect game with no hits and no runs. The Dodgers were shut out and the Yankees won! What a game!! It's funny that I remember nothing about the football game we went to see in Regina—but that baseball game was something else!

On the drive back to Yorkton, a new memory was made as Deany rested her head on my shoulder and nodded off. I experienced the wonder of smelling her hair and her perfume as she slept. I later found out the name of her perfume was "Here's My Heart"; appropriate since she stole my heart, and it has been hers since that day.

During this time, Deany's family was going through a crisis of their own. Her dad was experiencing memory lapses and terrible headaches that the doctor in Yorkton was not diagnosing correctly. It was later discovered that a brain tumour was to blame for these symptoms, and this was the beginning of his terminal struggle with cancer.

My love for Deany developed around church programs. We both remember an incident in the Sunday morning church service of the Yorkton Baptist church. The service was in English, but the pastor was Hungarian with a good command of German. His English, however, was still being developed.

One Sunday morning, Reverend Galumbus asked me to pray. It came out as: "Would the younger Schmell please pray."

My brother Jerry was the older Smailes and I the younger. The entire pew began to shake as the girls tried unsuccessfully to suppress their laughter about the younger "smell" being asked to pray.

We also sang in the choir together. I was encouraged to join because it was a good place to meet other young people. I had a good voice but only knew how to sing the melody. So, as a potential tenor, I would sit beside Elmer Schrader or Sig Mayesky, and try to impersonate their voices since I couldn't read music.

One incident we remember from choir occurred as we were coming down from singing to sit in the pews. One of the girls wearing high heels stepped on the heat register. Her heel caught in one of the openings, and she walked down the aisle with the register cover firmly stuck on her shoe.

As young people in a small city, our entertainment consisted of going to Broadway Avenue, the main street, on a Saturday night. We would park and watch people go by. This was in the days before television.

My brother and I were always active in sports, particularly baseball. We played on an organized adult softball team where I was a catcher and Jerry played shortstop. We could really play any position, and, when we joined the church leagues, we brought a level of competitiveness and excellence that made us popular.

Don pitching at church baseball game

Deany was not raised in a sports environment, so never became proficient at playing, but she learned to tolerate some of the sports.

Don and Deany talking through the window of Jerry's car

When I think back to my courtship of Deany, I am amazed that she not only tolerated me but even consented to be my girlfriend and later, my wife.

For her sixteenth birthday, I planned a fishing trip to York Lake. We left Deany's home at about five in the morning and arrived at the lake where we began to cast from the shore. We were using Len Thompson lures in the hope of snagging some northern pike or jackfish. The best vantage point was from the railroad bridge that went over a small narrow area of the lake. I managed to catch a couple of sixteen- or twenty-inch pike. Deany was a good sport about spending an entire day surrounded by bugs, smelly fish, and an eighteen-year-old suitor with questionable judgment. We still laugh about that encounter.

Deany's sixteenth birthday party (without the fish)

While getting to know Deany, I found a little field mouse one day, alive in a snowy pasture on the farm where we lived in Yorkton. My mischievousness won out over my better judgment, and I wrapped that pretty little critter up in tissue paper and put it in a can. I packaged it up nicely as a present and delivered it to Deany at one of her babysitting jobs where I sometimes had the privilege of accompanying her.

Deany opened the package, and upon seeing the mouse, screamed and threw the can in the air. The little rodent ran for cover as Deany hollered and ran the other way. I managed to catch the mouse and dispose of it outside, but I don't think I got any dates for a few weeks after that incident.

On another occasion, I was saying goodnight to Deany at her front door after an evening out in the wintertime. There was some snow, and, in my stupidity, I threatened to put some down her neck. She warned me that would not be a good idea. I persisted. She didn't slap me, but she quickly went in the house and slammed the door. I walked the mile and half or two miles back to where I stayed, shedding a lot of tears about how stupid a young man can be.

When Mother Ziolkowski was widowed, there was a pile of wood needing to be chopped up. During a period of time when Deany and I were at a difficult point in our romance, I went to the Ziolkowski home and spent some time in their woodpile. All that experience as a boy served me well as I chopped and stacked wood for Mother Ziolkowski. To this day, Deany says that my labours in the woodpile endeared me to her mother.

10. Bible School and Beyond, 1956-1957

When Deany's dad passed away, his funeral became the place I heard God's call to serve Him. At that time, the only people I had observed serving God were preachers, so I applied to Bible school.

I was accepted and went off to the Christian Training Institute (CTI) located between 108th and 109th Street on 78th Avenue in Edmonton, Alberta. This was my first exposure to a big city! I was assigned to a room in the student residence, and my roommate was Bill Thomas, who was also from a farm background. Being back in school was fun, although I was never much of an academic student. Socialization came much more easily to me than studying.

The school year went from September to May, and I enjoyed interacting with the other students. We were assigned duties to help run the school and to keep the costs down. I was responsible for shovelling snow and dish duty, which I happily did.

Playing tricks on one another was a highlight of living in community. A favourite prank was getting into someone's room and placing a can of water on top of their partially opened door so that when they came in and pushed the door open, they would be "baptized" by the upended can of water. I'm not sure this counted as a true baptism in church circles, but it was a lot of fun. There were community showers outside of our dorm rooms, and another favourite caper was throwing snow over the wall and onto the person having a shower.

The dining room tables were covered with oilcloth to make cleanup easy after meals. This waterproof covering meant you could pour some water on it and direct the flow down into someone's lap, making it appear they had wet their pants. A bit juvenile, to be sure, but these shenanigans made for good memories and a lot of fun.

With Bible school roommates. Don is on the left

One activity that I was very good at was crokinole. I became the CTI crokinole champion with my partner, Irma, who was the school nurse. She wasn't all that proficient at crokinole, but I was pretty good, and we managed to secure the championship title for our little school.

I also became part of publishing our school yearbook: The CTI Promoter. We corresponded with different churches who put in advertisements which offset the cost of publication.

One of the major emphases of the school was the music program. I enjoyed singing but was not disciplined enough to take vocal training. A song was assigned to me in music class, but I never got the chance to perform it there. The powerful lyrics and unforgettable melody of "Then Jesus Came"[2] still wells up from my heart often, and I sing it loudly to the only audience that matters!

In retrospect, I wish I would have taken more music training to develop that part of God's gifting in me, but I lacked the discipline and motivation.

During this time, I experienced a desire to bring together my early spiritual journey, which would be classified as Pentecostalism, with my current adventure in becoming a Baptist in practice. We were invited to visit North American Baptist churches in the area, and the closest one to us was McKernan. I frequented their services as well as those at Central Baptist which I enjoyed even more. We participated in some concerts there and perhaps even a mass choir. I also volunteered as part of my Christian education courses, teaching Sunday school in North Edmonton at what is now Northgate Baptist Church.

The first time I got to preach was at Hope Mission in the inner city. I was quite comfortable sharing the story of how I came to know Jesus. My dad's issues with alcohol also meant that I was not put off by the struggles of some of the people experiencing a rough life. I suspect my humble upbringing made me comfortable interacting with people in all sorts of situations.

Probably the thing I was most disciplined at during this time was writing letters to my sweetheart back in Yorkton. It was my first experience of communicating love and details of daily life by letter to someone I cared for so much. It was also the reason I was often in conflict with the school's lights out regulations, as I spent many a late night at the windowsill, pouring out my heart on the pages of a letter to Deany when I was supposed to be sleeping. Being away from the person I loved, with both of us being tempted by other relationships, was perhaps the most difficult part of my time in Bible school. Receiving a letter from Deany was the bright spot in any day.

I was able to go back to Yorkton for Christmas, and that reunion was memorable. I arrived at the Ziolkowski home and was waiting for them to return from a church service. Deany and her family drove up to the garage behind the house, and when Deany saw me, she sprinted across the garden—heedless of the snow—clambered over the fence, and ran into my embrace. I think she was honestly as happy to see me as I was to see her.

When April came and school was over, I had no job and no place to go. The school was expecting us to vacate the dorms, and I think some of us overstayed our welcome a little bit, but what can you do when you have no money and no place to go? While waiting for spring to come to Edmonton, I was able to dig some gardens for a few people to earn a bit of money.

I had recently become good friends with a fellow named Wolfram Leightenberger, and we had been corresponding with the Yukon Baptist Mission in the Yukon Territories. We decided to head to the Yukon for the summer, so on May 7th, we started out from Edmonton, hitchhiking.

Our first ride took us to the intersection of Highway 16 and Highway

43. A couple of young ladies gave us a ride as they were heading to their cabin on one of the lakes west of Edmonton. They dropped us off, and we had no place to go except into a nearby field. We tried to make a campfire but spent an uncomfortable night in that pasture. This prompted a prayer meeting where we asked God to provide us with transportation to Whitehorse. In the morning, we received a ride from a farmer to the Onoway corner.

Hitchhiking to the Yukon.

About fifteen minutes later, a car stopped, and it was an airman from the US Air Force.

"Where are you headed?" he asked.

"Whitehorse, "we replied.

"Jump in!" he said.

As it happened, he was stationed in Whitehorse, so some thirty-six hours later, he dropped us off right in front of the Yukon Baptist Mission. What an amazing answer to prayer for these somewhat foolish young men!

Whitehorse was wonderful! The mission was situated in some old army barracks that had been left there after the second world war. It consisted of an orphanage for small children as well as a school for First Nations children.

Mission Church and School in Whitehorse, YT

Whitehorse is located in a valley where the Yukon River runs through and is surrounded by large clay cliffs. The mission was right across the road from the recreational facilities of Whitehorse. This was my first exposure to the North, and in the summertime, it didn't get dark!

On June 21st, the longest day of the year, the sports ground would have a ball game that started at midnight, and you could play softball without any lights all night long. I had never experienced a place where you could read a newspaper in the middle of the night without any artificial illumination!

Our work there consisted of helping to maintain the existing buildings and pitching in on some new construction projects. They were building a new Baptist church in the Yukon, so we helped out with that as well as working with the summer camps held there for the young people.

At that time, I had no awareness of the residential schools that are a blight on our Canadian history. This school gave every appearance of being an extension of the kingdom of God to share the gospel with the people there. My understanding was that the Yukon Baptist Mission worked in cooperation with the First Nations community in that area to set up training that would serve them, and attendance at the school was completely voluntary.

It was wonderful to meet and interact with these Indigenous young people. I vividly remember one young man who was in the air cadets in the Yukon. As part of his summer experience, he travelled to Moose Jaw, Saskatchewan. When he returned, it was fun to hear his observations. He was flabbergasted by the difference between that part of Canada and the mountainous Yukon he had known up to this time.

"Oh, Don!" he exclaimed. "You can see nothing forever!!"

He had never seen so much flat land before.

That summer, the Yukon experienced many forest fires. One of these was started by the Air Force when they dropped some incendiary bombs in Lake LaBarge but missed the lake. The resulting forest fires near Whitehorse meant we had to evacuate the orphanage.

We took the small children to a place called Carr Cross. Most of the students were home for the summer, so they were thankfully not in the residence. There was a lot of smoke from the fire, and the ash dropped onto the roofs of the school buildings. We doused them with water to keep them from burning, and the smoke caused the city to be dark at 4:00 p.m., making it look like late evening.

I got to experience quite a bit spending the whole summer in the Yukon. Along the Alaska Highway and in some of the areas where the church was working with First Nation settlements, there was a lot to see. I was amazed at the purity of the water; you could see right into streams and observe fish clear to the bottom of the stream! I remember the beauty of the mountains; it was my first exposure to mountainous country, and I was awestruck.

One Sunday afternoon, I hiked up Grey Mountain outside of Whitehorse and was overwhelmed by the view from that height. Five thousand feet is rather impressive to a kid from the prairies.

Don and Wolfram in the Yukon.

Overlooking Whitehorse

The soil there and ground cover were all volcanic ash, and I remember being impressed by how flammable everything was. When an ember would fall into the ash, you could take that with some soil between your fingers to try and rub it out. You soon discovered how difficult it was to extinguish that spark. It gave me a deep appreciation for the challenge of fighting forest fires. I learned that the intense heat from a blaze can ignite a spruce tree five miles from the original site and cause it to burst into flames like a torch which would then start the inferno again.

Thankfully, God intervened in this forest fire, otherwise Whitehorse would likely have been incinerated. The wind changed, and the flames stopped their progression towards Whitehorse.

During this time, I also had opportunity to go up the Alaska Highway to mile 1016 where there was an experimental farm. I was amazed that they were growing wheat up in the Yukon and Alaska! With the twenty-four hours of daylight, they had at that latitude during the summer, the plants grow differently than in Saskatchewan where we had four months of summer, but no sunlight during the night.

Our reimbursement or remuneration at the mission was fifty dollars per month plus room and board. This was not enough to fund another year of theological training, so I began to investigate schools that would accept students on work scholarship. I was accepted into a school in Chattanooga called Tennessee Temple Bible School for my second year of theological education.

When our time at the Yukon mission was finished, I got a ride to Edmonton on a truck that was moving furniture and then hitchhiked from there to Yorkton for a quick visit with Deany. From Yorkton, I planned to hitchhike to Tennessee for the start of the school year.

All went well until my final ride to the US border. I was picked up by two Black men: one from Chicago and the other from Tennessee. This was really my first exposure to racial prejudice and the anger that can build up between different races.

During the fifteen-mile journey to the border, these men endeavoured to educate me by showing me at least six newspaper articles detailing the unfair treatment and racial discrimination experienced by Black people in America. As I looked at the articles and listened to the angry commentary of these men, I really had no idea what a volatile situation was brewing in that car and in the hearts of these individuals.

When we reached the border, the customs and immigration authorities would not allow me to continue riding with these gentlemen into the United States. I was compelled to buy a railway ticket to Chattanooga. I now realize that these border officials were probably God's provision to protect me from being dumped somewhere in the ditch by two angry Black men who were wrestling with their journey and not very fond of white people at that point in their lives.

The train ticket to Tennessee Temple cost almost all of the cash I had, and I arrived in Chattanooga with no money for the school term. However, I did collect some wonderful memories of going through places like Kentucky and seeing the beauty of the American landscape.

Arriving in Chattanooga was like entering a new world. That part of Tennessee is quite mountainous and has a tremendous history of the American Civil War. The terrain was beautiful, with mountains, forest, rivers, and farmland that was quite different from what I had experienced in the prairies of Western Canada.

When I arrived in the fall of 1958, Chevrolet and GMC were producing some amazing cars. I called the Bible school to let them know I had arrived, and they sent a 1959 Chev coupe to pick me up. I had never seen that kind of craftsmanship in a car before, and it was just brilliant.

At the Bible school, we were housed in apartments furnished with bunkbeds since there were three of us to a room. My two roommates were veterans of the school. They were in the college program while I was in the Bible school program and both had jobs in addition to going to school. One of them was on the school crew like I was, and the other worked as a tour guide for Lookout Mountain and the caves that were under the mountain. They were nice guys, and we got along just fine.

I had a picture of Deany on display, and on the picture was printed "Saskatoon, Saskatchewan" since that's where the photography studio was located.

Deany's photo from Saskatoon, SK

My roommates thought this must be a foreign language since they had never heard of such a place. We had many discussions about the differences between American and Canadian culture that further broadened our education.

I had never been to a church or school as large as the ones I attended at Tennessee Temple. The church had over four thousand members and sixteen out chapels which were like small church plants pastored by theology students.

The services were totally segregated, which was a bit puzzling for this farm kid from Canada. It was interesting to be in a culture where the people who worked in the kitchen and the people who did the janitorial work were Black, and didn't go to the same churches, or even eat at the same tables as the white people. They liked one another, but there was a definite separation that I had never experienced before. For me, people were people, and I could not understand the difference there.

The church services were amazing. I never went to a service either morning or evening where there wasn't a baptismal service. There were people coming to know Jesus and being baptized in every service, and it was quite astounding to me.

The professors were unique. There was one professor who was totally blind. He knew his Bible by heart and could quote the whole New Testament. You could give him a chapter and verse, and he would begin to quote the entire passage from memory. It was remarkable. His son was also a professor there and would lead his father from class to class for his lectures. His blindness didn't hinder his ability to teach at all.

The school had an amazing music program, and there was music coming out of classrooms and practice rooms all the time. There were orchestras and vocalists, singing groups and instrumentalists. They were all so professional! The assistant president of the school, Dr. Faulkner, had been a production manager for the motion picture industry before he was converted, and became a pastor and teacher. As a result, the musical productions coming out of that Bible school were often at a Hollywood level. As a young farm kid from Saskatchewan, I went around most of the time with my mouth hanging open.

The seasons were different in Tennessee from what I grew up with in Saskatchewan. That winter, there was snow; a unique occurrence! Most of the people at the school had never seen snow before. They couldn't believe that I came from a place where we often had snow seven months of the year.

There were students from Florida who brought back fresh oranges and grapefruit after spring break. I had never tasted a grapefruit before that was so sweet you didn't need to put sugar on it. It was an amazing time of having my horizons broadened by meeting so many people from diverse backgrounds.

One thing that impressed me was the American allegiance to their flag, and how that respect was reflected in the way they cared for the flag. I was assigned to put the flag up and take it down each day. Within the first two days, I was corrected and made to understand that the flag was never permitted to touch the ground, and that it had to be folded up in a particular way. This was absolutely new information for this Canadian who didn't come from a country where the flag was almost sacred in the way it was handled. The pride that American students had for their country was a lesson to me as a Canadian, and I respected that a great deal.

Coming from Canada, I couldn't receive wages in the US, and so I worked for the school forty hours a week to pay for my schooling in the work scholarship program. My assigned tasks included everything from scrubbing floors and toilets, to setting up for meetings and musical productions. I loved the work, and my boss was a great person. He taught me to add in my head by grouping numbers into tens and so going down a column of numbers to find the sum. I was amazed to find I could do this, and it was easier than using a calculator. I still do basic math that way, and as a result, am designated scorekeeper when playing games with my family.

I was assigned to serve a school that the church ran for the children of the community and also helped out in another program for literacy improvement. As I worked, I looked at every task I was assigned and sought to do each chore as if I was doing it for Jesus. This perspective still serves me and helped develop a strong work ethic. I truly enjoyed my work, and that impressed the people I was working for, and they treated me well.

The most difficult part of being so far away from home was missing my sweetheart. There were a lot of nice girls at Bible school—even some "Southern belles"—but the girl I loved was in Yorkton finishing her high school. Deany and I wrote letters during this time, but it sure took a long time for a letter to go back and forth between Yorkton and Tennessee.

I didn't appreciate how difficult it was for Deany not to have her boyfriend there to take her to prom, graduation, and other social events. What good was a boyfriend when he was half a country away? They say absence makes the heart grow fonder, but in this case, Deany's heart was torn, and she began dating other fellows who could accompany her to these social outings. As she was being romanced by these other guys, her letters to me became fewer and farther between.

One evening, I telephoned to remind her of my love and to talk through our relationship. We spoke for an hour and a half, and I'm not sure the phone company ever got paid for that call. I was expecting the call to be terminated when my money ran out, but somehow, we got to have a long talk.

I don't think Deany was convinced to stop dating other fellows and wait for me, but at least I was able to tell her that I still loved her. Even with the uncertainty of the future, I felt that God had His hand on my life and on our relationship.

One duty that fell to us as working scholarship students was stripping the floors of old wax and repolishing them. This had to happen at night when there wasn't the foot traffic that occurred during the busy school days. We would begin work at 5:00 p.m. and would finish at about 2:00 a.m., when we would have a quick sleep and begin class the next morning. As a young man, I thrived on this schedule. I was getting enough sleep, and I was learning things and being challenged.

While my work for the school paid for my tuition, I had no money for incidentals like toiletries and toothpaste. I brought this need to God in a prayer meeting, and His answer came in the form of a five-dollar-bill found in my blazer pocket. My friend Wolfram had put it there when we were still in the Yukon, and it turned out to be God's answer to prayer for me.

Recognizing that I had no money, the school allowed me to get a weekly job doing janitorial work for a camera shop in downtown Chattanooga. I would take the bus downtown, and this was another education opportunity for me. Integration was happening in the United States at this time, but the transition from racial segregation was not a smooth one. There were riots on buses as Black people sat in seats that had traditionally been reserved for white people.

I had never experienced any of these racial tensions and was quite naïve and ignorant of any potential danger to myself as a white person. There were many "coloured" people living in the areas surrounding the school, and I would go walking there without a thought. My American friends told me: "You can't walk there! It's not safe!"

But I never experienced any fear or sense of danger. Certainly, God protected me, and there was only one occasion I can recall when I encountered racial violence.

One of my friends from Pennsylvania and I decided we would climb Lookout Mountain one weekend. It was about a five- or ten-mile walk from the school, so we set out early one Saturday morning on our adventure. My friend had a speech impediment that often rendered him tongue-tied when he was excited or frightened. He also called everyone "Straw Boss," a term that was not intended as derogatory but could easily be misunderstood by those who didn't know him.

As we walked through the "coloured" section of Chattanooga on our way to Lookout Mountain, we passed a shop where a large Black man was working. My friend Don said, "Good morning, Straw Boss," just under his breath, perhaps as a reflex or maybe he was excited or nervous.

In any case, that big Black man came out of the shop, grabbed Don by the lapels of his coat, and began to shake him.

"What did you say? WHAT DID YOU SAY??" he bellowed.

My friend was struck dumb with fear, so I piped up, "He didn't mean anything by that!"

I received a punch to the side of the head, and we got out of that place quickly. I recount that story simply to illustrate the fact that racial tensions were a part of the culture there at that time.

We had one teacher in our Bible class who firmly believed in segregation. He was quite vocal in his disapproval about a student from India whose skin was the same colour as the African Americans, saying, "What is that Black person doing in our school? He should not be here in our class."

This made me so angry that I wanted to tell the professor, "Maybe you're the one who shouldn't be here!"

I wanted to remind him of what happened to Miriam and Aaron when they criticized Moses's wife who was a Midian. My understanding is that Midians were dark-skinned, and scripture says that Miriam and Aaron were struck with leprosy after their criticism. In my "righteous indignation," I may have wished for a similar fate to befall that professor.

While the cultural differences and racial issues were a difficult part of my time in the United States, seeing the natural beauty of that region was amazing. I had the chance to take a bus tour through Tennessee and the surrounding mountains. It was just beautiful! There were different types of hardwood trees that I had never seen before in Western Canada, and they produced the most spectacular fall colours. The water was strategically dammed up in places, and I learned that the Tennessee Electrical Society was known worldwide for their water management and hydro energy.

We went to one place where you could see six different states from the top of the mountain. God's creation is just amazing, and I think my eyes were as big as saucers taking in all this new scenery. We toured a lot of battle sites from the Civil War, and I was astounded to learn of the number of human casualties that resulted from this time in American history. There were old cannons and many beautiful memorials and parks to commemorate these losses.

While on this trip, I was showing a buddy how I could throw left-handed. I hurled a stone into the river, then watched in dismay as my watch came off and flew after the stone into the water. That watch was a gift from my brother Jerry, who had won it in a cattle-judging competition. It was worth about fifty dollars which was a lot of money back then!

I waded out into the river without stopping to take off my shoes, never letting my eyes leave the spot where the watch had gone. I reached down into the clear water and retrieved that watch, so grateful that God was looking out for me and the things that mattered to me.

I felt keenly the privilege of being alive to see and experience things I had never dreamed of before. My eyes were wide open to the wonder of God's creation and His goodness to me.

While I originally believed I was obeying God's call by going to Bible school, questions arose about whether there were other ways to serve God. Although my grades and school performance were fine, there was a deep desire to be discipled in more practical ways.

I sent a letter to Don Scott who had been the pastor of the apostolic church in Shaunavon when I came to know Jesus as Savior. I asked him if I could come and be his disciple, to learn about Jesus from him since he had been instrumental in leading me to faith as a child. I had so much respect for him and for his faith and character.

His response informed me that his situation had changed, and he was no longer a pastor. In fact, he was working in Medicine Hat at the ceramic factory there. Imagine a pastor leaving "the ministry" and working in a secular vocation! I believe this was the beginning of the realization that my calling really wasn't to be a pastor or missionary, but to serve God in other ways. I needed to find out why God had made me, and what He had made me to do.

In May when the school term was over, I was ready to go back home to Canada. I had no money for a train or bus ticket, so decided to hitchhike back to Prince Albert where my father and stepmother along with the second family were living.

My first ride was with some fellow students who were going back to Ohio or Iowa for summer vacation. They gave me a lift, and I enjoyed seeing a new part of the country in springtime. We encountered hundreds of ring-necked pheasants along the way; it was mating season, so they were quite active. I marvelled at these beautiful birds, saw the crops going in, and was struck again by what a rich and blessed country this was.

When I parted from these friends, I continued hitchhiking, walking, and carrying my duffel bag, trusting in God's care and the kindness of strangers. When you're hitchhiking, you don't have a lot of choice in your rides, but I generally made almost as good time as if I had been driving my own car. Sitting at the side of the road resting and waiting for a ride, I learned how to juggle stones to pass the time.

Somewhere in North Dakota, I remember feeling exhausted. It was late in the evening, and I saw an old, abandoned truck in a farmyard beside the road. I went over and that truck cab became my resting place for the night.

In the morning, I got up, had my prayer time, and went out to the road. Would you believe that the next vehicle to stop and pick me up was driven by a pair of fishermen heading to Lac LaRonge, just north of Prince Albert, Saskatchewan? I slept a lot those next twelve or fifteen hours, and awoke in front of my family's home in Prince Albert. God was certainly looking after me, and I was grateful.

11. Prince Albert, 1959

I had come full circle, ending up in the city of my birth some twenty-one years later. My immediate task was to find a job. Dad and Lorna allowed me to stay with the family in a home that was already crowded. A mattress was put on the floor for me, and my half brothers and sisters just scooted over to make room.

A blessing to the family was that I quickly obtained a job at the Burns meat packing plant. Burns had received a contract to deal with the surplus of pork at that time, and they were hiring people for the summer to process meat and support the regular workers. I was assigned to the day shift and would awaken early, walk the three or four miles from home to the plant, and get to work.

I was not a meat cutter, but I was a willing worker. Some of the work involved injecting brine into the hams and packaging them, and I did my best, even though I hadn't been trained in this. Soon, I was promoted to being a box maker, where I learned to run the machine that stapled the boxes together for use all over the processing plant. I set to work with my usual enthusiasm and soon had boxes stacked up everywhere. My boss had to tell me to slow down.

"Stop making boxes! We're not going to pay you for making more boxes! We don't need any more boxes!!"

This was my first experience working for a unionized work force. Union or no union made little difference to me, except that some of my pay was deducted for union dues. I was just happy to have a job. A nice bonus in working at Burns was that I got to take home meat at a discounted rate as an employee, and this was helpful to my family. I was happy that I could contribute to the running of the household and not be an imposition. There were five or six kids already in the family, and it was a busy house! I was looked up to by my half siblings, and I think they appreciated having a big brother nearby.

This time in Prince Albert was a precious time of reconnecting with my family. It provided a glimpse of the challenges that Lorna, my stepmother, was facing as she dealt with the reality of raising kids and having very few financial or practical resources. Dad was struggling to maintain gainful employment, partly due to his lifestyle and also due to the residual effects of his horrific fall mentioned earlier. The family was living on welfare and doing the best they could in those trying circumstances.

What amazes me now is that when I get together with these siblings, I see people who learned how to fend for themselves in a dysfunctional situation and grew up to be fun-loving, hardworking, responsible members of society. The poverty of their childhoods, while it affected them, did not define them. Although they grew up with an alcoholic dad, they also remember a dad who coached their baseball teams and was there for them, as well as a mom who did the best she could for them, and loved them deeply.

It was during this time that I became aware of an area of neglected hygiene in my life. I had only been to a dentist twice in my life at that point: once as a six-year-old to extract a tooth that was growing in the wrong place, and once as a twelve-year-old when half of a tooth had been knocked out by a hockey stick, and the other half had to be removed. I did not have the habit of brushing my teeth, and the idea of oral hygiene was foreign to me. I may have thought that if I did start brushing, those teeth would start to come out! I don't remember anyone ever complaining about my breath, but I certainly had several gaps where a toothpick would go right through. Teeth were there to chew, in my opinion, and since I never had any trouble eating, I wasn't much bothered by my teeth. I always said that if I got a bad toothache, I would see about fixing my teeth.

One Friday night, I got a toothache that lasted all through the weekend until Monday morning. It was bad enough to interrupt my sleep, so on the way home from work on Monday, I stopped at the dentist. There was an assessment, and I went through the procedure of having all my teeth removed. The dentist observed that there was really no point in trying to save any of the teeth, since they were all in pretty bad shape and likely to fall out anyway. I had gum disease as well, which further exacerbated the situation.

The solution was to take out all my teeth, a quarter of them at a time. So, for the next two weeks, I would stop at the dentist after work on Monday and again on Friday, they would put in freezing, remove a quarter of my teeth, and send me home to recover. Most of the teeth popped out pretty easily, but I will never forget the final extraction. The other teeth had been pulled with little to no pain because of the freezing, but apparently the enervation of this last tooth came from nerves on both sides of it. As a result, the freezing didn't have the same effect, and when the tooth came out, I came up out of that dentist chair too. It felt like having a tooth pulled with no anaesthetic, and I had never experienced anything like it.

I normally have pretty good coagulation, but for some reason, this last tooth extraction caused me to bleed all night long. Even the next day at work, I had to continually swallow or spit blood. On the way home from work, I stopped in at the dentist, and he sent me to the hospital. I walked there and was given an injection in my bum. Whatever they injected was really viscous, almost like glue, and I felt it going through every fibre of my gluteus maximus muscle. I limped home, groaning with every step. It was not a process I'd want to repeat.

However, the bleeding did finally stop, and Lorna was able to wash the blood out of my pillowcase. I spent two months without teeth while my gums healed, and then was fitted with my first set of plastic teeth (dentures). The whole procedure cost two hundred dollars with all the extractions and the new dentures. I was so grateful to have earned enough money at Burns to not only put food on the table, but also pay for my new teeth.

One amazing thing that happened during this period was that I received a letter in the mail that had gone from Yorkton, Saskatchewan, to Chattanooga, Tennessee, and back to Prince Albert, Saskatchewan.

This letter was from the girl I was in love with, and she had experienced a change of heart. She wondered if we could be reconciled and continue with our relationship. It didn't take me ten seconds to write a reply: YES!!! I was the happiest toothless person you had ever seen! Deany's change of heart occurred when she was stricken with rheumatoid arthritis in her senior year of high school. She had to be hospitalized and was in tremendous pain, unable to walk or carry on with her normal life. During this time, I believe God reawakened her feelings for me, and that was the best news I had received in a long time!

12. Swift Current, 1959-1960

My employment at Burns was coming to an end, and as I wondered what to do next, my brother, who was living in Swift Current, told me of an opportunity there. I packed up and headed on to my next adventure. It was 1959, and my first job in Swift Current, Saskatchewan, was helping a machinery company build a warehouse. I really had no building expertise, but I did have some muscle and a willingness to work which got me the job.

One of the things they had me do was move a large excavator, which was bigger than any tractor I had ever driven, from one place to the other. I probably should have had some instruction or training before undertaking this, but I didn't. As a result, I learned some things the hard way—like the fact that when you took your foot off the gas, the vehicle didn't slow down. You had to gear down and apply the brakes. Going at highway speeds and then making this discovery, I ran off the road and drove the tractor through the ditch. Thankfully, there was no damage to the machinery, and I learned from the experience.

That job lasted for about a month, and when it finished, I got a job in the meat packing plant. I just couldn't get away from livestock and meat production. Not that I was too sad about that.

Treen Packers was my next employer, working for Jerry and Shorty Treen, two brothers who owned the business. My work was primarily packaging meat, moving it around the packing plant, and serving customers. During this time, I got to see how sausage is made using mostly scrap meat, fat, and seasoning. It's a marvel that I still love it, but I really do! I came to truly appreciate meat cutters while working here.

Our meat cutter's name was Joe, and he was masterful with a knife. He had escaped the Hungarian Revolution in 1956. We joked that you didn't want to get him drunk when he had a knife in hand, since meat might not be the only thing he could cut.

I started golfing in 1959 or 1960 in Swift Current, Saskatchewan. Some of my colleagues in Treen Packers were golfers, so I went to the local store and purchased my first set of golf clubs. They were a Spalding

Starter Set and cost $39.95. They included the golf bag, a driver, a 3-wood, and 5 irons including a putter. That set of clubs served me for twenty years, so it was pretty good.

The golf course in Swift Current is located along a creek, probably Swift Current Creek, and the first tee box is located up on a hill. I teed up my golf ball and took a mighty swing as if I were playing baseball. I missed the ball and staggered, almost falling down. On about the third attempt, I topped the ball, causing it to roll down the steep hill. My work colleagues probably still laugh when they recall this outing. It wasn't until much later that I got some tips from other golfers that may or may not have improved my game.

My brother Jerry and I lived together in a little one- room apartment. Our favourite lunch was a sandwich of cheddar cheese and strawberry jam; not gourmet fare, but I still enjoy this combination for almost any meal.

Jerry had a Rambler car, and one of our favourite activities in winter was hunting rabbits at night in the moonlight. We would chase them in the car, shoot them with shotguns, and throw the carcasses in the trunk. We didn't eat the rabbit but didn't waste the carcasses either. We sold them as fox feed to people who raised foxes for the clothing industry.

These trips over rugged terrain were not the best medicine for a car, and Jerry's vehicle developed a leak in the gas tank. We took it in to get repaired, forgetting that there were a bunch of dead rabbits in the trunk. When the trunk was opened to access and fix the gas tank below, the discovery was made that one of the rabbits was still alive. It jumped out and, evading the grasp of the mechanics, ran several laps around the shop before making its escape. This became a great story in town with people saying, "You can't trust those Smailes boys with anything!"

Jerry (L) and
Don (R) on
Jerry's car.
Rabbits,
beware!

I connected with the Salvation Army church in Swift Current while living there and even got to preach once. I remember my sermon was on being God's sheep and how sheep aren't really that smart. The sermon was somewhat autobiographical since my life has provided many examples of the Shepherd's mercy in the face of some pretty foolish actions.

There was a young lady at the church that I was attracted to, and I began to court her. I hadn't resolved my feelings for Deany, but started to date this other girl, Melody. As we got to know each other, her heart became attached to me, while I realized that Deany was the one I really loved. I took a walk with Melody to share my heart and, after walking a couple of miles, realized that this was a terrible way to break up with someone. The two-mile walk back to her home seemed much longer with a heartbroken girl sobbing all the way.

During this time, my relationship with Deany continued to evolve, albeit at a distance once again. She was in Edmonton at the Christian Training Institute (CTI) where she was upgrading her high school marks that had been affected when she was stricken with rheumatoid arthritis. It was during this new chapter in her life that she decided to go by Gerry rather than the "Deany" of her youth.

She was in a singing group at the college, and I discovered that they were going to perform in Medicine Hat, Alberta. My love affair with this girl had developed to the place where I knew she was the woman I wanted to marry. I had already gone to Smith's Jewellers where I spent a lot of money on an engagement ring and was just waiting for an opportunity to "pop the question."

I went to Medicine Hat and enjoyed the concert, but discovered, to my dismay, that the girl I loved was also dating other guys! My heart was broken, but not beyond repair. I realized that if I was going to have a relationship with Gerry, absence would not make her heart grow fonder towards me. I went home pondering what would become of my romantic life.

I continued to work at Treen Packers but knew that this was not my future. My brother was moving towards his marriage to Donna Faber. Her family lived on a farm about an hour outside of Swift Current, and we often visited there. When Jerry and Donna married in June of 1960, I had the privilege of standing up for them and welcoming a wonderful sister-in-law into the Smailes family. Their happiness further convinced me that I needed to pursue a relationship with Gerry with both of us in the same location.

13. Edmonton, 1960

After Jerry's wedding, I resigned from Treen Packers and made my way to Edmonton. I didn't have a job there, but had made contact with my friend Wolfram Leightenberger, so at least I had a place to land in my new city.

I started out working odd jobs and trying to sell encyclopedias with Wolfram. I lived in a rooming house, and one night awoke to someone going through my clothes in the closet. I pretended to still be asleep to avoid a more serious situation with the intruder and tucked a kitchen knife under my mattress the next day for protection.

Gerry was working at the university hospital in Edmonton and suggested that I also try to find employment in one of the hospitals. On August 2nd, I went to the Royal Alexandra Hospital for an interview and began work as an orderly the very next day. There wasn't the same training and orientation they now have for new employees, so I just jumped in to learning on the job.

I was amazed to be working in a healthcare setting, since I had only been in a hospital twice before in my life: once as a six-year-old having my tonsils removed and then as a teenager visiting my father after his accident. Neither of those experiences had been pleasant, but this was a new chapter in my life, and I was excited and ready to learn.

My first assignment was to the orthopedic ward. I remembered having a cast on my arm when I had sprained my wrists while at school in Beatty, but the patients in this ward were in much worse shape. There were a couple of patients that I still remember quite vividly.

Mr. W was an elderly gentleman who was a poet. I don't remember why he was in the orthopedic ward, but he was a very happy man and was often quoting poetry.

Another patient had been in an accident in the oilfield. Something had fallen on his leg and crushed it so badly that it had to be amputated. We had several conversations, and he was determined that he would ride a motorcycle again. I was intrigued by this and admired the attitudes of these men.

My duties were as varied as the patients I served. The nurses were my bosses, so I did what they told me to do. This was the first time I had ever had female supervisors besides my mom and some teachers, but I really had no trouble submitting to their authority. They were amazing at what they did, and certainly knew much more about patient care than I did. They taught me how to use wheelchairs safely, how to lift and move patients who were immobilized in casts, how to empty bedside urinals, and even how to give enemas. Sometimes, I was taught by other orderlies who had presumably been taught by the nurses or someone with more experience.

The gentleman who taught me how to prepare an enema lathered some soap and warm water, scraping off the suds into a receptacle of warm water that had a hose attached. The hose was inserted into the anus of the patient, and the warm soapy water was poured in as an enema. I had never seen or experienced anything like this in my life, but I remembered it because it was the only instruction I was given on administering enemas.

A few months later, I was transferred to a surgical ward where a patient was being prepared for bowel surgery. My instructions were to "give enemas to clear." I had no idea what that meant, and, in the absence of further clarification, I gave two or three enemas to the patient, thinking that was fine.

The next day when the patient went to surgery, the surgeon was not happy with the condition of his bowels. I don't think the patient suffered too much from my oversight, and the staff were very gracious about my mistake, but I learned that "clear" meant something different than what I had produced.

I loved the hospital environment and learning to interact with people who had different needs. My supervisors had to tell me: "Go have your break! Go eat your lunch!"

I would get so involved in learning and serving, that I would forget about everything else. It was very fulfilling to help people, and I think my attitude and demeanour were appreciated by those with whom I worked. I don't remember a patient ever being cross with me. I had a strong, able body from doing physically demanding work, I learned new things every day, I was appreciated, and I was paid for my work. As my wages accumulated, I opened a bank account. Life was good.

Shortly after this, I had my first experience with someone who had left their body and graduated to eternity. A patient had died, and I was asked to prepare the body for the morgue. Again, I had no instruction, and this was the first dead body I had every touched or encountered that I could remember. This person had an indwelling catheter. In the absence of any instruction on catheter removal, I simply pulled the catheter out. Thank goodness the person was dead, since a live patient would certainly have complained!

I discovered that a catheter is held in place by a little balloon on the end of the tube which is inflated with saline once it's in the bladder to keep it from falling out. When removing a catheter, you have to first deflate this balloon by letting out the liquid, and then the catheter slides out easily. This was a timely discovery since soon after this experience, a spot opened up in the urology department. I applied and was accepted, graduating from orthopedics to urology.

My supervisor, John, was a veteran of the Second World War where he had served in the Polish Army as a medical attendant. He was a good teacher and understood that this young farm boy needed to be taught about healthcare. I thoroughly enjoyed my relationship with John, and quickly learned how to care for people who had urinary tract issues.

What I enjoyed most about working in the urology department was the scope of learning, as we served patients throughout the hospital. It was very exciting when the urologists did cystoscopies or transurethral resections.

We would prepare the patients for these procedures, and occasionally, the urologist would allow us to look through the cystoscope. Viewing the bladder with all of its intricate vascular anatomy was astounding. We would often see a white orb the size of a golf ball, and the urologists would discuss how to remove it. Despite the cliché of doctors spending a lot of time golfing, a 9 iron would not do the trick on a golf ball of this sort. Watching the stone be pulverized and removed, or seeing obstructions in the urinary tract excised by cauterization, certainly heightened my interest in healthcare.

14. Settling Down

Life outside the workplace revolved around time spent with Gerry. My living conditions had been upgraded to a small basement room of a private home, and Gerry and I took the bus back and forth to spend time together whenever we weren't working. My days of travelling here and there to find a job were over, and I was feeling settled in Edmonton. The more time I spent with this girl, the more I realized that I wanted to marry her. We were in the same location, and as I observed her life and sampled her cooking, I was determined to share life with her. The engagement ring was already in my possession; all that remained was to "pop the question."

One day, Gerry was pressing my shirts while I lay on my bed; this was as much practical as comfortable, since my one room barely had space to walk around when the ironing board was in use. I looked at this amazing girl, and marvelled again that she loved me enough not only to spend time with me, but also to press my clothes.

"Would you be my wife?" I asked from my prone position.

"Ok," she replied, "but you didn't ask my mother."

"I didn't know I had to," I countered. "I didn't realize I was marrying your mother."

I now understand that marriage joins two families, so I was very willing and happy to make the phone call to Mother Ziolkowski. She graciously gave her blessing which meant the world to me, and so began a wonderful relationship with a very special mother-in-law.

Despite the unromantic proposal, Gerry was excited to begin planning the wedding. We didn't see any reason for a long engagement; we were anxious to begin a life together. Gerry was able to use her sister Artrude's wedding dress which fit just fine, and the wedding was set for February 4th, 1961. We asked Gerry's cousin, Eunice, and my brother, Jerry, to be our attendants.

We had to look for a new place to live, since Gerry's apartment was still occupied by her cousin and was not suitable for a couple of newlyweds. My little room by the furnace was even less suitable. We found a small basement suite on the south side of Edmonton that consisted of a little kitchen, living room, and bedroom. When you splashed water in the bathroom, you could read the newspaper that was under the paint! There was a metal shower with a small curtain located out in the common basement area behind the furnace. There was no place to get undressed there, and it was necessary to go past the stairway that led up to the back door in order to reach the shower. You were never too sure if the landlord or some other voyeur might get an eyeful when you made the dash to and from the shower, so showers were a bit riskier than we might have wished. Still, the suite cost us thirty-five dollars per month, and we figured that two could live as cheaply as one, so we rented our first home as a couple.

The timing of the wedding in the middle of winter did not conform to the usual practice of summer celebrations planned around school and work vacations. As a result, most of our family members were unable to attend. In fact, several of our married sisters were pregnant and unable to travel for the wedding. Our brother-in-law Richard Grabke came to visit, and in his direct way asked whether our haste to marry was because we were pregnant. We assured him that was not the case. There may have been others who wondered the same thing, but we were just anxious to start a life together and saw no reason to wait any longer. After falling in love with this girl four years prior, I felt we had waited long enough!

The wedding took place at McKernan Baptist Church, and the day was a special gift from God. February 4th was so mild that year that you didn't even need an overcoat, meaning we were able to go from the car to the church without any adverse weather conditions.

My friend Wolfram Leightenberger was good with a camera, so he became our photographer. Our friend June Snyder was the soloist, and Reverend Alphonse Lamprecht was the minister.

It was a beautiful ceremony, and when I saw my beloved bride coming down the aisle at 2:30 that afternoon, my heart almost exploded. She was absolutely gorgeous, and I felt like I had been blessed beyond anything I could imagine. There were only twenty people at the dinner, so it was a good deal for Mother Ziolkowski, as the bride's family traditionally paid for the wedding.

Mr. and Mrs. Smailes. Edmonton, AB, 1961

The reception was held at the airport motel where we also spent our wedding night and honeymoon. The wedding was on a Saturday, we had Sunday off as our honeymoon, and Monday we were back at work. I still marvel at God's amazing provision of this beautiful woman to be my wife, my life partner, and the mother of our children.

No matter how much one reads about marriage or how many relationships one observes, married life is a very personal adventure and life experience. In every way, I have to admit, I was naïve, ignorant, and even thoughtless at times. I was unprepared for the changes occurring in my life, having gone from being independent and self-reliant to joining a family that was close-knit and very different from what I had experienced. I had a lot of growing up to do.

While I continued to work at the hospital, Gerry was working as a proofreader for a small publishing company called Sun Publishing. This was located on the south side of Edmonton, and we both relied on the bus to get to work. It wasn't long before we realized that we needed a car. Our first automobile was a yellow American Motors Rambler. My brother helped us with financing in the form of a loan, and I chose this car simply because Jerry had been driving a Rambler. We soon came to realize this vehicle had been placed on the used car lot for a reason: true to its bright yellow colour, it was a lemon. We were never able to go more than 100 km from the city without it breaking down. We soon disposed of it and purchased a 1958 Volkswagen Beetle from

Edmonton Motors, a more reputable automobile dealer. This was a good little car and served us well.

Having reliable transportation in place, we set about moving to a second basement suite with more room, located a few blocks from our first place. Our new landlady was gracious, and for sixty dollars a month, we enjoyed much more space.

One cold winter day as Gerry was coming home, she discovered a tiny kitten huddled in a footprint in the snow near the entrance to our suite. The little creature was mewling piteously, and no one with even half a heart could have left it out in the snow. Gerry rescued the kitten who provided much delight and entertainment as our first pet.

If we forgot to close the door to our suite, the little cat would go upstairs to the main level, run across the floor, and climb up the sheer curtains. Our landlady was visually impaired, and before she could figure out whether this creature was a rat or something else, the cat would be down the curtain and back in our suite. I don't recall if she ever did find out that we had a cat since we had not asked permission before adopting the little fellow. We were of the belief that it was easier to ask forgiveness than permission.

This kitten was very playful, and when you moved in bed, it would jump on you and scratch you. I ended up with scratches on my hands from our little tussles which didn't really bother me.

One day, I came down with a fever, and Gerry was confronted with a husband who was covered in sweat one moment and shivering hard enough to shake the bed the next. She piled on as many blankets as she could to keep me warm, but when my temperature went up to 105 or 106, we went to the emergency department of the Royal Alex Hospital where I worked. I was admitted immediately and placed in a ward where they packed me in ice and started IV antibiotics. The diagnosis was blood poisoning, which must have resulted from me handling infected urine in the course of my work duties after being scratched by the cat. We had no idea of how to deal with a severe fever like that, and Gerry remembers being shocked when they were packing me in ice. We were certainly grateful for medical expertise and this intervention. After two days in hospital, the antibiotics had done their work, and I was back to normal.

While I continued to thrive in my work at the hospital, Gerry was not fulfilled in her job. She met a lady at work who was looking for a homemaker to prepare meals and look after her home, as well as someone to do home maintenance.

Betty lived in the east end of Edmonton, and we moved into a beautiful basement suite in her home on 50th Street. Gerry took over the duties of running the home. Part of our responsibility was also looking after her black poodle who, we discovered, really ran the home.

This dog had the habit of urinating all over the house wherever and whenever he chose to. He was so used to having his own way that he would take a dishcloth and not allow you to take it away from him; he had never been trained or taught to obey. I was not about to tolerate a dog who thought he was the boss.

The culminating event happened when the dog went down and peed in our apartment. I came downstairs, interrupting him, and he was not happy. He sank his teeth into my hands, and I battered that dog with my bare hands until he was almost unconscious. I then took him for a long walk for both of us to cool off. I don't think he ever dared to set foot in our basement suite again, and I was thankful we didn't have to stay in that situation forever.

We spent two years living and working at Betty's place, and that time prepared us for the next phase of our married life. I enjoyed doing the yard work, and Gerry was fulfilled being the amazing cook, caregiver, and homemaker that she is. Our proximity to the hospital was a blessing as I could come and go from work without spending too much time commuting.

*Don and
Gerry as a
young couple*

One holiday season, I had to work on December 25th, and the idea of eating Christmas dinner alone didn't appeal to either of us. Gerry came to the hospital, and we got our dinner in the cafeteria to eat in the respiratory department. When you're young and in love, even the simplest celebrations are wonderful as long as you can be together.

During that time, I got up one morning and went out to get in the car to go to work. The only problem was that there was no car. I have been known to forget where I've parked on occasion, but this was different: our car had disappeared overnight. We reported it to the Edmonton police, and a day later, the car was found abandoned in another part of the city. It had been broken into and stolen. Thankfully we had no valuables in the vehicle, and it was still in fair shape when it was found.

That little car had a few mishaps over the course of its time with us. Driving to work one morning as I crossed the Dawson Bridge, I glanced down at the river, and in that split second, my Volkswagen attempted to mate with the car ahead of me which had stopped for no apparent reason.

On another occasion while coming home from work on 95th Street, I was stopped in traffic behind a gravel truck. When the traffic didn't move, the gravel truck backed over my car. Thankfully, he stopped before crushing me in the driver's seat, but the poor car met with some damage. I think that VW was too small for people to see it, and as a result, it sustained some injuries that were not all related to my questionable driving ability.

It was during this period that my sister Patricia was married to Don McMillan. The wedding was to be in Kenora, Ontario, and my sisters Phyllis and Lynn, who were living in the Northwest Territories, came to Edmonton to travel to the wedding with us. We loaded into our little VW bug with a car-top carrier that was almost the size of the car itself and made the trip to Kenora, ON.

Our little VW loaded up and Ontario bound.

How that little car made it all that way is a miracle and a tribute to German engineering. With the accelerator pressed to the floor, it would only do sixty miles per hour going downhill and forty-five miles per hour going uphill, but it made the trip.

This adventure was one of the chapters in our life when Gerry gained an understanding of the weird and wonderful family into which she had married. When we arrived in Kenora, we discovered our sleeping accommodations were little more than an air mattress in a broom closet. On reaching the wedding venue, my sister asked me to give the toast to the bride. That wasn't a big problem for me, but Gerry had never been in a family where someone would be asked that at the time of the event. In her family, that request would have been made six months to a year before the wedding.

As we were trying to sleep that night in our little broom closet, Gerry expressed to me her amazement bordering on disdain for how the wedding was planned. In the midst of this conversation, an ironing board that was hanging on the wall fell down and hit Gerry on the head. We dissolved into fits of laughter as it seemed the good Lord was correcting her for an attitude that perhaps needed adjustment.

Grandma Pearl, my mother's mother, was in attendance at Pat's wedding. As I gave the toast to the bride, I recounted a story from our childhood on the farm in Beatty. I told how Pat had pushed me during an argument, causing me to hit my head on the coal scuttle, almost knocking me out. Grandma Pearl spoke to me after the toast saying, "Patsy would never do that!" It's wonderful how saintly we can be in the sight of someone who doesn't see our everyday behaviour and experiences.

After Pat's wedding, we returned to Edmonton and our life there. Soon we decided it was time to begin our family, and Gerry began the amazing journey of motherhood. It would have been wonderful to have her sisters or mother nearby to share insights and provide support for her during this time, since she had little help from her husband. She managed, however, and on March 17th, 1964, three years after our wedding, the first addition to our little family arrived.

15. Parenthood and Family Growth

I didn't have a lot of training before becoming a parent, but my beautiful bride Gerry and I ended up with some children coming into our home. When Gerry began to have labour pains with our first child who was expected on March 17th, 1964, she woke me up saying, "I think it's time to go to the hospital."

It was 4:30 or 5:00 in the morning, and we were still living in our basement suite at Betty's house. We navigated the mostly empty streets and went to the university hospital where Gerry was admitted. I dropped her off and went to work. In those days, the husband really didn't have a lot to do with the birth of a baby besides the genetic contribution and taking the labouring woman to the hospital.

At about 8:00 a.m., our beautiful little girl arrived, and since she was born on St. Patrick's Day, an Irish name was in order despite her German and English heritage. Kelly has had to cope with green birthday cakes ever since.

A phone call alerted me that my daughter had arrived, and on my way home from work, I went to the hospital to meet the new addition to our family. My first view of this little miracle of creation was through the window of the nursery where I spied a little bundle in a bassinet. I was overwhelmed with a mixture of joy and wonder as I pondered this new responsibility.

The nurse brought Kelly to Gerry's bedside, and I got to discreetly watch as mother and child bonded over the giving and receiving of nourishment. I had never seen that before, and it was amazing to witness God's design in this tiny human. I even got to hold this little one. Thus began my journey as a dad.

After a week or so, Mom and Baby were discharged to come home, and we were on our own as new parents. Mother Ziolkowski came to help us for a while as she did with each of the children's births, and we were grateful for the gift of family.

The day after Kelly was born, I had to navigate the custom of handing out cigars as a new father. Because I was a respiratory therapist in the making, smoking was not something I necessarily wanted to encourage. Besides, cigars were pretty stinky in my opinion! I think I bought a few Havana cigars to satisfy the die-hard smokers, and then a bunch of black licorice cigars and pipes for the rest of my friends. I handed these out to my colleagues at the hospital and enjoyed the congratulations, good wishes, and words of advice showered on a new dad.

Our basement suite in Betty's northeast Edmonton bungalow was a wonderful home. Kelly's arrival coincided with Betty falling in love and marrying a doctor. We were happy for her and felt that it was time for our little family to move on to a new place.

Our next home was a one-bedroom apartment on Tower Road North; it was still a basement apartment, but its location was close to the hospital which made getting to and from work much easier for me.

Kelly was easy to care for and we were lulled into the belief that parenthood wasn't so difficult. There was a lot of joy in our little home as Gerry fell into the role of motherhood quite naturally. Mom and Baby got into a schedule of eating, burping, and sleeping with very little struggle.

We had a couple of memorable visitors during this time: Gerry's older brother Erwin was working on a master's degree at the University of Alberta and came to visit us. He took great joy in interacting with Kelly, and in retrospect, he was probably missing his own family at the time.

The other amazing visitor we had was Grandpa Smailes (my father's father), when he was on his way up to Hay River to visit Phyllis and her family. He had been recently widowed and wanted to visit extended family. We have a cherished picture of him smiling as he held Kelly in his arms. That turned out to be the last picture any of the Smailes had of him.

As Kelly grew, her favourite activity was bouncing in the Jolly Jumper. We attached this contraption in the doorframe of our bedroom and enjoyed hours of entertainment as Kelly bounced and laughed and made us laugh in turn. Who needed TV?

Our apartment was very near the municipal airport which meant there was no shortage of planes taking off and landing. I don't recall being bothered by the noise, but when Kelly began to talk, one of her first sentences was: "Look at the plane!"

Another favourite phrase as Christmas neared was: "Look at the lights!"

It was evident she was going to be gifted in areas of speech and language, as she loved to talk.

Since parenting is a learn-on-the-job endeavour, the firstborn has the job of breaking in the new parental recruits and putting up with their mistakes. In our case, Kelly was a fairly easy-going, compliant child who was eager to please. Lest we become complacent and overly confident in our parenting skills, God varies the dispositions of our children so that the next lessons we need to learn come in the second or third editions. This has a way of ensuring that parents get a well-rounded education.

When Gerry became pregnant again, we knew we would need more space for our growing family. We investigated and found a two-storey rental near the Misericordia hospital. The complex was designed for low-income families who could qualify for a rent subsidy based on their income. It was wonderful to have three bedrooms as well as a living room, kitchen area, and even a basement! We moved in just before Terri was born and were very appreciative of the extra room.

I don't have a clear recollection of getting Gerry to the hospital for Terri's birth, but I suspect it was similar to the first birth experience. I dropped my lovely wife off at the hospital where she was already familiar with the whole procedure. Later that day, I got to meet our beautiful new daughter Terri.

Kelly was delighted with her little sister, and the two girls enjoyed lots of playtime together. Terri definitely had a mischievous streak and loved to laugh. There was lots of joy and fun in our household as the girls entertained each other and their parents.

We didn't have a lot of time to fear the future or to feel like we were in over our heads in this adventure of parenthood. We tried to live in the moment and kept busy with work, taking care of the kids, being involved in church and community activities, and just being a family.

Early family trip to SK

Moving to the West End of Edmonton, we began attending Meadowlark Baptist Church on 156th Street and 90th Avenue. Friends who attended that church also lived in the same rental complex, so we had the joy of seeing our children play and grow together. This church community became home and a wonderful place to develop spiritually through services, Sunday school, and rich friendships that endure to this day.

I recall an incident when I was trying to build something that would allow the kids to sleep in the back seat of the car while we drove to visit family in Saskatchewan. Apparently, I was engrossed in the project and didn't notice that it was after 10 at night. Some neighbours came out and shouted at me to "knock it off!" Working in the hospital for ever changing shifts, I wasn't always aware of what time it was and needed reminding that some people required sleep at night in order to work the next day!

Our trips to Yorkton in the wintertime were an adventure. It seemed like it always either rained and froze, or that we had snow to contend with on the journey. Small cars are fun to drive, but they sure are hard to keep on the road in those conditions. We would almost always end up in the ditch and needing to get towed at some point during the trip. It was only God's providence and a very patient wife who loved to visit her family that kept us making this pilgrimage back to Saskatchewan. It helped that the kids would sleep as we drove, and God looked after us.

As our girls grew, most of the responsibility for training them fell on Gerry. My involvement was as the authoritarian person; I expected the children to do what they were told and particularly to obey their mother. Kelly was very compliant, so we really had very little trouble teaching her. Terri was much more strong-willed, with a mind of her own. One occasion that stands out in memory was while Terri was being toilet-trained. Gerry was out for some reason, leaving me in charge of the kids. Terri was put on the potty to do her business and sat there for quite some time. When she was allowed off the potty, she scampered behind the chesterfield where she proceeded to poop on the carpet. It only took one spanking, and she never did that again. I doubt Dr. Spock would approve of this method of potty-training, but we found that our second daughter needed a more hands-on approach to know where the limits of her freedom and her parents' authority were.

Perhaps one may wonder how we learned to be parents. I came from a background where we were just trying to survive much of the time. I lived in a community and culture where many of my friends and other families had similar challenges during that time after the war. As a result, I really had no training in being a dad. Obviously, that didn't stop me any more than it stops most people who embark on the adventure of marriage and parenthood. We just learned on the job as it were. The wonderful thing about marriage is that you don't have to do life and family alone. As the Bible says, "the two become one" (Mark 10:8), and thankfully Gerry had a healthier family experience from which to draw. She took to being a mom very naturally, and since we lived at a time when the father's role was seen to be more that of a breadwinner, I worked hard and left most of the parenting and child-rearing to her.

At the end of the day when I came home from work, it was a great joy to hug my wife and to hold my children. I would help feed them, watch them play, and help put them to bed, often taking time to read to them. We got into our little family routines, and the kids grew up strong and healthy.

My main responsibility was making sure our family was cared for financially, providing for their physical needs, and I was able to do this through work that I enjoyed. We didn't live a life of luxury, but we had enough, and Gerry was very good at economizing to stretch our income. Gerry looked after most of the daily needs of our children, and she taught them how to behave. My role was making sure the kids respected their mother, and they knew that if they didn't obey her, they would have to deal with me.

Since I didn't have much in the way of examples in how to raise children in a God-honouring way, my "parenting manual" became The Christian Family by Larry Christianson[3] among other books popular in the evangelical mainstream at that time. Nowadays, embracing a philosophy of corporal punishment could land someone in trouble with child protection agencies, but at that time, spanking was accepted as a normal part of raising obedient and respectful children.

God worked in my heart, and I don't ever remember punishing our children in anger. If you knew my dad and his capacity for rage, you would see what a miracle this was. I don't remember the kids needing many spankings since seeing a sibling being disciplined would often be enough of a deterrent for bad behaviour in the other kids. I do recall that when giving a spanking, I was often crying as much or more than the child receiving the punishment. I hoped that my tears would communicate the broken heart of God when His children choose behaviour that is harmful.

In fact, Kelly attributes her Christian conversion experience to an incident when at seven years of age, she was being punished for some misdeed. Neither of us remembers the exact transgression, but on this occasion, I was talking with my teary-eyed daughter after the spanking to make sure she understood why she had been punished. I asked if she would like Jesus to help change her heart. Perhaps some of the motivation for praying was based on a reasonable desire to avoid further spankings, but Kelly experienced a rebirth into the kingdom of God, and I was humbled to be part of such an important event in her life.

I never thought much about controlling or planning the additions to our family. That was more of a concern for Gerry since she was the one who would be most affected by a pregnancy and would bear most of the responsibility for child-rearing. We didn't spend a lot of time talking about having children. Nor did we worry too much about whether we could afford to have a family. I had a good job, and we made do with the income we had, paying our bills and making what we believed were responsible decisions.

We didn't have credit cards back then, just a paycheque and bills to pay, so we lived simply within our means. As the kids grew, Gerry sewed their clothes, and we benefitted from hand-me-down clothing from friends and family which helped with our budget. Gerry was very good at economizing and running the household, making sure we were all fed and clothed.

I was ignorant of the stresses of motherhood, because Gerry seemed to handle our children very well. However, we were not intending to grow our family beyond the two daughters God had sent. Somehow, despite taking precautions to prevent pregnancy, Gerry discovered she was expecting again. Having two children under the age of four and discovering there was another on the way was a lot to take in, and there was perhaps not the same excitement over a new addition to our family at first. However, as her pregnancy progressed, we eagerly anticipated the arrival of this little miracle.

When Gerry went into labour late in the afternoon on February 10th, 1968, we went to the hospital. Her labour went on most of the night, and I was allowed to sleep in a chair in the waiting room since I didn't have to work the next day. When Evan was born, two days after Terri's second birthday, we definitely felt like our family was complete.

Gerry remembers that Evan didn't cry immediately after he was born, and as he was taken away to be examined and stimulated to breathe, she was filled with angst. She worried that something might be wrong with this little one whose arrival had not been as anxiously anticipated at first. Finally, a loud cry assured her that her son was equipped with a fine set of lungs. As it happened, Evan Todd was a very contented baby, and we were all so grateful that God overruled our attempts at contraception.

By this time, we had progressed enough in our earning ability to purchase our very first home. In 1969, with loans from Mother Ziolkowski and my brother Jerry, we became the proud owners of a three-bedroom house on 90th Avenue in the West End of Edmonton. With school and church nearby, it became a great place to raise our three children and make good family memories.

Happy mother of three!

Storytime with a lap full of blessings

When our children were in elementary school, we lived very near the school, so Gerry was even able to provide before and after school care for other kids in the neighbourhood whose parents both worked outside of the home. Our home was also across the alley from the parsonage where the pastor and his family lived.

When we were attending Meadowlark Baptist Church, Rev. Bert E. Milner was our pastor for many years and baptized both of our girls. A favourite memory of that time was when Evan engaged Pastor Milner in conversation one afternoon.

"What's your name?" Evan asked.

"Bert," he replied.

Evan looked at him and burst out laughing. Being an avid fan of Sesame Street, Evan had never considered that a pastor could have the same name as a Muppet character on TV.

Evan always brought humour and laughter to our home. He was happiest running around outside with his friends, riding his bike, building a fort, and enjoying the freedom of being a kid. His sisters would sometimes take advantage of his easy-going nature to dress him up with an old wig of Gerry's and include him in their tea parties, but he was definitely all boy despite his long eyelashes.

We enjoyed family camping trips—an inexpensive vacation which made for great memories enjoying the natural beauty of our surroundings. There were also plenty of trips to see extended family in Saskatchewan. Birthday parties, friendships, softball teams, hockey and skating in winter—these were the simple pleasures that filled our days as a young family.

16. A New Profession

Meanwhile, back at the hospital, I began to realize that while I enjoyed the environment of healthcare, I wanted to pursue something that would be a career instead of just a job. An opportunity to become an air traffic controller came my way. I applied and soon received notification that I was number two in the Edmonton area to go to Ottawa, Ontario, and begin training. Proverbs 16:9 says, "We can make our plans, but the Lord determines our steps." (New Living Translation) On reflection, I believe God intervened in the form of our prime minister, Mr. John Diefenbaker, being faced with having to balance the budget. The air traffic training program was deferred, and would you believe that at the same time a new program of respiratory therapy was being piloted at the Royal Alex hospital? I applied and was accepted as the first student in this new program.

A major healthcare change was occurring in Edmonton. The old Royal Alex was being closed, and a new hospital was being constructed across 111th Avenue. As this hospital was being prepared, a fledgling profession was being introduced. The profession was so new that it did not even have an established name.

In Canada, it was called "inhalation therapy," and in the United States it was called "respiratory therapy." The beginning of this field came as a result of the invention of compact intermittent positive pressure breathing (IPPB) apparatuses used to support high altitude flying. These were called ventilators or respirators. They had been used in the medical field to assist patients who were in intensive care units and were found to be much more effective than the previously employed negative pressure breathing apparatuses like the iron lung. The most notable usage of the iron lung had been in the treatment of polio patients.

This new respiratory equipment had arrived on the scene and needed people to care for it and apply it to patients. The equipment and its maintenance were often organized under a department of anaesthesia, internal medicine, or thoracic chest specialties.

One of the first major programs in Alberta originated at the university hospital under the direction of a talented young man called Dr. Brian

Sproule. Mr. Klaus Becker, a graduate of this program, came to the Royal Alex to be the director of inhalation therapy. Mr. Becker was a passionate man of German heritage who had been a telephone technician in his native Europe before coming to Canada. His passion to build a profession was intense, and his desire to be the best was contagious.

I remember vividly my first interview and meeting with this man who was to become so influential in my life. We met at the coffee shop in the new hospital, and in my unassuming jovial way, I addressed him as "Klaus" during the conversation.

"My name is Mr. Becker," he informed me.

I could almost hear the umpire call out "Strike one!" and resolved to address him less casually in future.

My ignorance of a new profession was profound. On my first day in this new job, the hospital was still in the construction phase. We really did not have a curriculum, and the training was going to be intensely practical and "hands on" as we learned by doing. My first visit to the new department was impressive. Everything was brand-new and freshly painted. There was lots of room, but no patients yet. Instead, there was tons of equipment that needed to be categorized, labelled, and put in place.

I really knew nothing about the respiratory system. I knew nothing about disease. I knew nothing about anything that happened in the hospital other than my limited experience of inserting catheters and doing whatever I was instructed to do to help sick people. This environment was totally new, and I had never had a boss like the one I now had.

My first tasks were more like what you would expect in a machine shop for someone training to be a mechanic or lathe operator. Coming from my previous work caring for patients, this was a bit anticlimactic, but I was optimistic that my training would lead to patient care.

The workroom was equipped with a metal lathe where we turned aluminum rods into heating elements for nebulization. You must realize that I had never even heard the term "nebulizer" before, and as I cut aluminum rods with a hacksaw, it took some imagination to believe this had something to do with patient care.

Klaus Becker was a great teacher. He had an amazing ability with technical tasks. Those eight-inch aluminum rods were put on the lathe to be trimmed down, then onto the drill press to be hollowed out. Finally, electrical elements were put into them and screwed on. We made these components because to buy them would cost two hundred dollars per heating element, whereas, with some sweat, calluses, and technical ability, we could produce them for ten dollars apiece.

The hospital was planned by architects and people who knew nothing of the new inhalation or respiratory therapy. In all the hospitals at that time, if a patient needed oxygen or suctioning, you brought in an oxygen cylinder or a little electrical machine to suction out secretions. The new reality in this cutting-edge facility was that oxygen and suctioning ability were piped into every room with outlets built into the wall above the patient bed. Earlier designs featured thirty patients in a ward, with a smaller capacity area where patients could be moved if they needed suctioning or oxygen support. However, since all the respiratory equipment ran with compressed gas and was required at every patient's bedside, the new hospital was built to have that gas piped into each bed.

Before we knew it, we became consultants for the Misericordia hospital which was also being built at that time. They wanted to avoid that oversight in construction in order to keep up with the advances in respiratory therapy. It was an exciting time even though we were not yet treating patients, since we were getting hospitals equipped and outfitted to accommodate the new treatments this young profession would require.

Our technical training sessions involved taking a piece of equipment and learning how it was made, how to take it apart, and put it back together. We had to understand why it was needed, how it was to be used, as well as how to clean and care for it. Regulators were the primary equipment used to control pressure in the gas cylinders we used in the breathing machines to aid respiration. Regulators also controlled how much suction was applied to clear secretions from the breathing passages. The main therapies used were oxygen therapy, and inhalation of different medications to treat airway diseases and to prevent complications after surgery. Everything was brand-new, and it was an amazing place for this Saskatchewan farm boy to find himself.

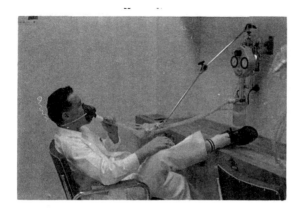

Don trying out some respiratory equipment

The training program at the Royal Alexandra Hospital for inhalation therapy, or "respiratory therapy" as it was later called, was intensely practical. We incorporated the knowledge we gained into daily work. It was the first time I had experienced an educational approach like this, and I thrived on it. The reason I was able to take this training and still support a family was that the hospital continued to pay me the same wage I had been earning as a nursing orderly. I was so grateful for the opportunity to learn a cutting-edge profession, to apply the training to work experience, and to still provide for my family.

There was really no curriculum written down on paper for the new program, and there were only three students in the first class: me, Ron Soderberg, and Jim Tiffin. We were a unique combination of personalities. Ron had a tremendous ability to organize things, while I was good at performing tasks. Jim had giftings in both of those areas but had the additional responsibility for a wife who was carrying twins in a complex pregnancy. Ron's wife was an ICU nurse which greatly helped our program with access to knowledge and insight we might not have otherwise had.

One of the first things we did as students was to contact other respiratory training programs that were operating in the United States. Many of these faculties were very gracious in providing us with their curriculum. We modelled our program primarily after a program in Grace New Haven Hospital in Connecticut where a Dr. Egan was in charge. He had written a book called Respiratory Care that became our manual.

Our academic training involved taking anatomy and physiology courses as well as other subjects at the School of Nursing. We would attend classes there in the mornings with the nurses and work afternoon shifts in the hospital. Once the intensive care units were established in the new hospital, we would sleep in the room beside intensive care, getting up every hour to check on our patients. It was an interesting experience.

Once we passed the basic curriculum of anatomy and physiology, we received lectures from physicians on respiratory and cardiac physiology and function. We had lectures from pharmacists on the pharmacological part of our treatments, as well as lectures from pathologists on the pathology of the diseases we were treating. Every area that touched on respiratory, including anaesthesia, was incorporated into our program.

In reflection, I believe this kind of experience and training was ideal for a fledgling profession. We had access to other programs for comparison and resource sharing, and we had great cooperation from our hospital administration and medical staff. As a result, we flourished as a department.

The test of any training program really comes down to examination, and, in our case, we were being critiqued and examined every day in the work that we did. Our medical staff loved the program, and we were well accepted at that level for the tasks we performed. There was some early opposition from the nursing staff because we were now a profession that contributed towards and interacted in patient care. However, that resistance quickly dissolved as the nurses saw the benefit of our contributions and we learned how to work as a team.

The introduction of intensive care medicine was a progression in our training program that came later. At this stage, the Royal Alex had been primarily a teaching hospital with a tremendous volume of patients being admitted, treated, and discharged after successful treatment. This emphasis on learning undoubtedly made it the ideal place for a new profession to thrive.

The passion of Klaus Becker to be the best department in the world, especially better than the university which had failed to hire him as their director, was transmitted to us as students. We had a strong desire to be the best. As students, we found ourselves able to visit other centres to provide service and training. The delineation between being a student and graduating to become part of training new students as well as providing service in the hospital was blurred, since we continued learning even after completing the program. This was only the second or third respiratory program in the whole province, and there was always something new to learn as the respiratory profession took shape.

I will always be indebted to the Royal Alex Hospital and the people there who helped form me into a caregiver. God built the desire to care for people into my personality, and having the freedom to develop and learn with very few limits was truly a gift. We were confronted every day with problems and challenges in patient care, and our work environment allowed us the freedom to come up with creative solutions. It was a wonderful setting, and the motivation to be at work every day was extremely high. I was so focused that I often had to be told to go home at the end of a day. This excitement carried a genuine risk of imbalance between work life and my role as a husband and father.

I mentioned before that the technical aspects of our program were taught on the basis of the equipment we were using. One of the challenges we discovered was the effect of our climate on respiratory conditions. In our cold winters, the air one takes in has very little moisture content, and warming it up requires a lot of humidification, either from the respiratory system itself or from external humidification. Our hospital was not built to support extreme humidification, and before the pediatric pavilion was constructed at the Royal Alex, we had rooms where we set up central humidifiers to run all the time. This was particularly helpful for children with croup and various upper respiratory tract infections.

These devices constantly broke down from so much use, so we learned how to repair them rather than replace them. The technical ability to modify or repair machinery became part of our training and daily experience. I am very grateful for that since I had very little prior exposure to that type of work and was able to become at least somewhat proficient with practice.

The Royal Alex was very gracious and generous in allowing us to go on trips to other hospitals that had made advances in treating certain conditions. I was privileged over the course of my training to go to the Children's Hospital in Chicago, stopping by The Hospital for Sick Children in Toronto en route to see how they were managing pediatric patients on ventilators. This was very helpful in bringing back information to our own hospital to improve our practice.

Ron had the privilege of going to the Winnipeg General Hospital where they were using a similar kind of ventilator as we were, and they had developed a technique of having the inspiratory and expiratory cycles modified to better manage patients in the intensive care units.

As I was finishing my training, the Royal Alex allowed me to spend a couple of weeks at the university hospital participating in the care of patients receiving cardiac surgery and some residual polio patients since we had no cases like this at the Royal Alex. This was another example of how accommodating the hospital was, and it was immensely helpful to my training.

There was a gentleman at the Royal Alex who was being treated for Marfan syndrome. While encountering him on rounds, I learned that the condition was genetic and that it affected the connective tissues of the body. The most serious complication of this was that the arteries lacked the necessary elasticity to return to the appropriate size after dilating to accommodate blood flow. The aorta tended to balloon up and would eventually burst in an aneurysm leading to death.

I happened to be at the university hospital when this same patient was transferred there for surgery, and I had the privilege of observing that operation. The aortic artery was the size of a big piece of bologna and the surgeons had to taper it down to a place where they could repair it. The time the patient was on the heart-lung machine was the longest that had been experienced up to that point in that kind of surgery, and I got to watch the procedure. To add to the story, months later, I saw that patient crossing Jasper Avenue by the General Hospital, recovered and in apparent good health.

Years later while in Toronto for a conference as part of our home care company, I conversed with the taxi driver who drove me from the airport to my hotel. He confessed that he had been diagnosed with Marfan syndrome and that he feared he might not survive. I told him of this patient with the same diagnosis in Edmonton who had recovered after surgery, and, before leaving his cab, I was able to pray for him.

Two years after this encounter, at another conference in Toronto, one of the staff recounted a story about a man with Marfan syndrome who had recovered after a successful surgery. Upon further investigation, I found it was the same taxi driver I had prayed for two years prior.

It was this kind of experience that I lived day after day, seeing God take the little bit that I knew, and using my willingness to serve to impact the life of another person. I learned that the things God allows in your life are never wasted or accidental. Certainly, my journey in respiratory therapy is full of such stories.

The proof of how effective a training program is must be assessed at some point by national examinations and accreditation. During the time I was there, the Royal Alex never had a failure in the Canadian registry examination, and in fact, boasted two gold medal winners for highest achievement in the country. I certified as a respiratory therapist in 1965, and soon thereafter was promoted to the assistant director of respiratory at the Alex.

The next year, in 1966, I challenged the American registry for respiratory therapy, because I wanted the freedom to practice my profession across the border if opportunity allowed. My written exam was arranged in the Edmonton office of Dr. Aaron, who was a member of the American Thoracic Society. He oversaw my written exam.

At that time, the pass rate in the American registry was something like 23 percent, which might have unnerved me had I known that statistic beforehand. It turned out that I had time not only to finish the exam but also to write down the questions to take back to our department at the hospital. I don't remember what my mark was, but I passed the written test and was able to go to Los Angeles to complete the oral portion of the exam.

This was a wonderful experience since I realized that our program at the Royal Alex was of the same calibre as any institution in the United States, and I was gratified to have confirmation of the quality of our department and hospital. I was successful in passing the oral evaluation and had the added bonus of watching the Los Angeles Dodgers play in Dodger Stadium. What a treat that was!

Having both registries opened the door for employment in the United States. My fellow students from that first respiratory class went on to success in the profession as well. Ron Soderberg transferred with his wife to California, where he introduced respiratory into some hospitals there, overseeing some of the training, and eventually getting into the home care business. Ron's life was cut short, but he made a tremendous contribution to my life and to the profession of respiratory therapy.

Jim Tiffin went on to become the first director of respiratory at the Misericordia hospital after graduation, introducing the program in that location. His real passion, however, was to become a pastor, and he later became an Anglican priest, entering the ministry together with his wife in the Anglican church.

The Royal Alex continued to take students and train them in hospital as respiratory therapists. The Northern Alberta Institute of Technology (NAIT) eventually started a program in respiratory therapy, taking the training of respiratory therapists to a whole new level. The partnership between NAIT and the hospital meant that students would take classes at NAIT and be trained practically in the hospital at the same time.

Those of us who had been part of the early days of the profession considered the responsibility to train new students a privilege. I had opportunity to teach some classes at the School of Physical Medicine at the university where I talked about the therapies we administered and how the different respiratory machines worked. It was a wonderful experience of learning—and not just for the students!

Smaller hospitals would also send some of their nursing staff to be trained with the equipment, and many of these hospitals were run by the Catholic Church. Interacting with the nuns, or "sisters" as they were called, was a joy. It was a time of breaking down religious prejudices in my life as I saw that these sisters loved Jesus just like I did.

I am so grateful that my experience in healthcare was not just a journey of treating cardiorespiratory diseases, but that it taught me to enter into someone else's health problems in a way that could bring comfort and healing to the person as a whole. It was very fulfilling.

17. Practicing the Profession

Don Smailes, RRT, in uniform

School does not end when one completes the training program. Being one of those privileged to participate in the beginning of a profession, we can think we know something. However, time often reveals that what we thought was true knowledge was not as comprehensive as we first believed. True knowledge requires practicing the profession, and I'm so grateful that the learning process continued throughout my respiratory career.

The new profession was very active, and we had the opportunity to contribute in various ways. The Canadian Society of Inhalation Therapy Technicians was established, and the first convention was held in Edmonton. The name was changed to the Canadian Society of Respiratory Therapy, and I have a recording of my lecture in that first conference. I discussed how to establish a respiratory therapy department, and hearing myself expound on what little I knew is humbling. When you have a little bit of information on a topic that has not been widely studied, you are considered an "expert" in the field. The truth was that I still had a lot to learn.

We had the privilege of starting and publishing the professional journal for the society. The idea was birthed in the hospital coffee shop and, before I knew it, I was the managing editor of this publication. I actually got to write a couple of articles, one on "What Constitutes a Professional"[4] which attracted the attention of Dr. Brian Sproule, who was in charge of the respiratory program at the university hospital. He called to congratulate me on the article which was a huge encouragement. All a farm boy needs is a pat on the back now and then to be stimulated to do all kinds of things.

My second article detailed the cytology practice we had developed to induce sputum specimens.[5] We had the patient breathe highly humidified air for a time, which induced a productive cough, enabling us to collect sputum samples to send to the lab in order to diagnose various respiratory conditions.

These were all wonderful opportunities to grow, and I soon found myself serving as a board member of the Canadian Society of Respiratory Therapy. In this role, I was privileged to travel all over Canada for meetings, seeing the Maritimes for the first time and other beautiful parts of my native country.

There were ample occasions to develop leadership skills that come with responsibility and opportunity. I'm very grateful for that and often say that the ability to speak and lead may not even come from your profession. In my own case, much of that was developed in the local church, where I was working in things like Sunday school as superintendent, in Boys Brigade, and as a deacon or board member.

Looking at my journey in respiratory, I can see where God in His providence had already placed me in circumstances and situations that formed me into a person who was suited for the profession of respiratory. I don't classify my life into segments of vocation and other things; it's a total configuration of a life where all these things work together. Certainly, my experience in respiratory and other areas confirmed the truth of this, and that will become apparent as the story continues.

When promotions came, my responsibilities changed. I found that my life was becoming less about interaction with patients and more about learning administration, problem-solving, staffing issues, dealing with government, budgets, and learning how to relate with other departments in the hospital. This was a tremendous opportunity for growth. Courses and training were provided by hospital management to help me navigate these new challenges, and I had no idea how this experience was preparing me for the next chapter in my life when I would leave the Royal Alex.

One of our duties as respiratory therapists involved resuscitation: the attempt to restore life to a person who had quit breathing. We were trained, and we trained others using a mannequin called Resusci-Ann. We had to do airway management, breathing, and cardiac compressions. In the hospital, whenever anyone was discovered having a cardiac arrest or breathing cessation, a Code One was called. We would stop whatever we were doing and run to that patient.

As respiratory therapists, we became the chief resources in a resuscitation attempt. We became expert at airway management and at compressions, using a bagger to "breathe" for the patient and trying to revive them. Before we had resuscitation bags to breathe for a patient, we learned the technique of mouth-to-mouth resuscitation.

One of my most memorable experiences came when I received the call and went to respond to the emergency department. On reflection, the person was probably dead on arrival, but we tried to resuscitate. I remember doing mouth-to-mouth on a young boy of ten or twelve, and having his stomach contents come back up into my mouth. I didn't suffer any ill effects from this, and we were not successful in resuscitation, but I will never forget realizing that the boy was the same age as my son, Evan. This impacted me in a powerful way. Even now, I tear up, realizing how life can end in a moment. I was being transformed to understand and treasure this gift.

One of the things occurring during this time without any plan or analysis, was the formation of a community around me. When you enter a profession at its inception, leadership is not an option; it just happens. Our team at the Royal Alexandra Hospital became much like a church fellowship. Respiratory therapy wasn't just the way in which we made our living; it became a calling and focal point for our lives. Some of the most long-standing friendships and relationships were formed in the respiratory community. My children speak fondly of my work colleagues who became uncles and aunts to them because our lives were so closely connected. Two families in particular have remained a big part of our lives.

The Wallace Tarry family became very special, and we remain close friends. Colin entered the program as a student at about the time I was in my second year of respiratory. He transferred from Fort St. John, BC, with his soon-to-be wife Carol who was an RN, and joined the program.

Colin had unique training and history in that he was raised in England by a father who managed a tea plantation in Ceylon which is now Sri Lanka. Colin's schooling took place in private schools where he learned to do all kinds of sports, and everything really, in the correct way. That was the opposite to my growing up where I learned to do things, including sports, just because that's what we did for recreation. Somehow, God, in His providence, put us together and the friendship just developed.

When Colin was going to marry Carol, she went home to Ontario ahead of time to prepare for the wedding. Colin needed to get from Edmonton to Ontario to join his bride for the wedding, and I had a new Rambler car. I realized that Colin needed that car more than I did at that time, so I loaned it to him. He drove nonstop to Ontario for his wedding and then drove back with his new bride after the festivities. That's the kind of community we were.

Colin taught us how to really fish for trout. Neil Patterson who had been a part of the Jasper Park ski patrol was another fishing enthusiast in our group, and the two of them organized an annual fishing derby for our team. We would go to Geraldine Lake, up from Athabasca Falls in Jasper National Park, where we would camp, hike, fish, and tell stories. It became an entire respiratory department event, and we have photos of some of our graduates carrying some of the female students piggyback over streams to get to the fishing holes. Those kinds of experiences really cemented friendships and relationships.

When children came along, we shared those experiences too, and rather than typical baby gifts, it became the common expectation that when you had a baby, you got diaper service from the department. We were just that kind of family. Almost every weekend it seemed like somebody was moving, and we all pitched in as colleagues to help one another because that's what friends and families do.

Some other close friends, Lorne and Linda White, met when Lorne was taking classes at the school of nursing as part of his respiratory training, and Linda was a student nurse. They fell in love and got married and have been a big part of my life.

18. Hunting and Fishing and Golfing, Oh My!

Lorne's in-laws were amazing hunters and outdoor enthusiasts, and that opened the door to fishing trips I had never dreamed of before. Fishing on the Bow River in a little canoe with a motor, and powering up against the current, then drifting back down was a wonderful way to spend a day. We would catch twenty-pound mother rainbow trout and then release them. I remember being in the river, trying to keep the fish on my line from taking off downstream, while Lorne was trying to get a net under the fish and bring it into the boat. Wrangling a twenty-pound trout on a four-pound test line and trying to keep the fish from snapping your line is no mean feat! It was like a rodeo on the end of a fishing pole!

We also enjoyed some hunting expeditions because Lorne's father-in-law had a swamp buggy with gears that allowed us to go anywhere in the bush. If we ran into trees, we either cut them up or ran over them and let the vehicle do it for us. I had a real British .303 army rifle that was the kind my dad had used as a soldier in the Canadian Armed Forces. Gerry had bought it for me as a Christmas present. I took it hunting for deer and moose, and once for a bear as well. I had been out hunting before but didn't know where to shoot an animal.

One cold morning while hunting with someone else, I had stopped to "drain my radiator" as it were. My rifle was propped up against a tree, and while emptying my bladder, I looked up to see a great big doe watching me. She had no shame, spying on a man engaged in such a private activity! I quickly and quietly finished up, took my rifle, and wondered where to shoot this animal who so obviously wanted to be harvested. She was very close, but I didn't want to ruin perfectly good venison by shooting in the wrong place. I was zeroed in on the head, then shifted my aim slightly down the neck before pulling the trigger.

The .303 threw me back about a foot, as the deer reared up on its hind legs and ran off. I went over to where it had been standing and picked up a coffee can full of hair, thinking it was probably God's providence that I didn't kill that deer. I had gone hunting with a friend and his son. The man had a hunting licence, but I naively thought I could just pick up a licence at a service station on the way. There were no licences available, and, had I shot that deer, I probably would've been caught by the warden and penalized. It did teach me that if you're going to go hunting, you should at least know where to shoot the animal.

On one trip with Lorne White and his father-in-law, Raymond, I asked where a deer should be shot. Raymond replied that you should aim just behind the front shoulder; about a foot or eight inches below the spine.

The next time we went out hunting, I had a licence, and as we rounded a corner, there stood a magnificent buck, waiting for us. I took what I had learned from my mentor, fired the shot, and the deer collapsed. When we skinned the animal and harvested the meat, we saw that my shot had hit the top of the heart, causing it to bleed out perfectly. I got some good venison steaks from that, and Raymond used the hide to make beautiful gloves for his family.

Later that day, we saw something black further down the trail and thought it might be a moose. It went into the bush, and I followed to get a better look. What should I behold but a mother bear and her yearling! I had not expected this and for a moment was at a loss. The bear was behind some willow bushes, and I worried that a shot might be deflected by the willow and just aggravate her. I wasn't sure if I could climb a tree faster than she could. As if to give me a clearer shot, the bear began to climb a nearby tree, and I shot her right through the heart. She fell from the tree and, as I approached, I realized this bear was probably six feet long from nose to tail and must have weighed five hundred pounds. The rest of the hunters came, and we pondered the dilemma of how to get the animal home since we were quite a distance from our vehicle.

We decided to skin the bear and then take the meat out in parts. This was probably November or early December, and the bear had most likely been in hibernation but had come out of its den due to the warmer weather. The hide was unbelievable—thick and luxurious enough to bury your face in; it was a prime hide. I had no idea that a bear is more like a beaver than a muskrat when it comes to its hide. I was familiar with skinning muskrats, but a bear hide has no meniscus between the skin and the meat. There's just fat growing on the meat and attached to the hide. We wanted to keep the head of the bear attached, so we cut from the underside of the chin and tried to remove most of the meat while not damaging the hide. We did take a hind quarter of the meat since we wanted to taste it, and we carried this bear hide about a mile out to where we had the Land Cruiser and swamp buggy and loaded it up. I took the bear back to Edmonton. My dad was staying with us at the time, so he helped skin it. We took the hide and had it processed, including the head, and it became a rug in our home.

We used some of the fat, since someone told us it worked really well to fry doughnuts, so we tried that. We also ate some of the meat and found it to be surprisingly sweet. I expected it to taste like beef, but it was totally different and quite unique. Years later, we made a gift of that bear skin to an Inuit family from Grise Fiord, NWT. Our daughter Kelly was involved with a cultural exchange in 1979, and the people from the north had never seen a black bear before, only polar bears. It seemed like an apt gift to foster good will and education.

These were the kind of experiences born of the friendships we formed in respiratory. Another adventure that involved Lorne White and his father-in-law took place during a fishing expedition on the Kakwa River just south of Grande Prairie. I had a canoe which Lorne and I had loaded up with all our fishing gear, gold pan, and supplies. We planned to drift down the river and meet the others in two days at a pre-arranged destination downstream where they would pick us up. We didn't know the river, but that didn't dampen our enthusiasm in the least.

We set out drifting and enjoying good fishing that consisted of mostly trout and other small fish which we threw back. We had gone in to shore at one point and then went out again in the canoe, fishing the whole river. There was a place where the river divided, and we followed the mainstream which, in retrospect, was probably taking us backwards.

As we rounded a bend drifting backwards, we saw a log jam that was about thirty feet long. We had life jackets on and decided our best bet would be to jump out of the canoe when we hit the logjam, pull the canoe up out of the water, and portage across to the other side of the logjam. I was successful in doing this, but Lorne was not. As I jumped up onto the logs, Lorne ended up still in the canoe as it began to float under the logjam. He passed by where my body was still hanging off the logs and was able to grab onto my legs and launch himself out of the canoe. The canoe went under the logjam, and most of what we had with us was lost, but we were so grateful that Lorne had not been lost. Had he not been able to grab my legs, his lifejacket would have certainly caused him to be trapped under the logjam. Having these adventures and living to tell the stories made for deep and abiding friendships.

In later years, I found great pleasure working with Ralph Sperry in home care. In addition to being co-workers, I became a member of the Sperry family which added another rich facet of joy to my life. The Sperry's had a farm in the Bashaw area where they allowed me to plant a bit of a garden. They also had a slough where we could shoot muskrats—as they say, "You can take the boy out of Saskatchewan, but he's still going to want to shoot things!"

One memorable occasion involved taking our friend Ken Tin, who hailed from Hong Kong, and teaching him how to shoot muskrats. Despite his prior army training, hunting small rodents on the edge of a slough required a different type of marksmanship. He took up his position on one side of the slough, and I, the experienced muskrat hunter, stood on the other side.

I shot a muskrat, but only caused him to lose some teeth before he swam to the other shore. Ken saw his chance, but never having shot anything so small and active, he fired and fired and fired again. I was beginning to be concerned for my own safety as well as the muskrat when God directed the little rodent to swim back over to my side of the pond.

As he approached, I fancied that muskrat pleading with folded paws, "Please will you harvest me and get it over with?!" When Ken and Ralph and I get together, this story still evokes rounds of convulsive laughter as we recall the comedy of that experience.

Muskrat harvesting occurs in the spring when the hide is still valuable for making coats and apparel. As a result, you are often hunting when there is still ice on or under the water. I was taught that anything you shoot should be useful and to not harm animals just for fun. Imagine shooting a muskrat that has a value of $1.75 for its hide, but it happens to be in the middle of a slough that has ice on the bottom. In order not to waste what you have shot, you take off your pants and wade into that cold water up to your nipples to get that hide. That's the story of muskrat hunting in Alberta and Saskatchewan where even a grown man becomes a boy again with a gun in hand and muskrat in his sights.

Gardening at the Sperry's farm was amazing. I loved being able to plant a garden much like I had back on the farm but now in the company of my new friends. I remember arriving at the farm to harvest my carrots and potatoes on a day when Gordon Sperry, Ralph's father, was combining. I was able to become once again the twelve-year-old boy who drove the truck from the combine to the granary, started up the auger, and emptied the truck into the granary. What made it even more enjoyable was hearing my new friend comment: "Isn't it amazing that a respiratory therapist came out to be my hired man!"

Later, when I went to dig the carrots and potatoes, I was excited about the harvest since my carrots looked full and healthy on top. When pulled up, however, they were half eaten. Apparently, the resident moles were delighted with the vegetable buffet I had grown for them.

Golf was another arena for developing friendships and learning not to take myself too seriously. My friend Harry Zeitner and I found ourselves in Nelson, British Columbia, in July one year golfing and curling. We loved it when our schedule allowed us to curl in the evening, leaving the daytime free for golf. We were playing a course, and I was having a difficult time. My ball was going everywhere, and my distress was evident to my friend Harry.

He said, "Don, I don't usually like to give my opponents information, and I really don't like to coach someone else as if I have all the answers, but I have noticed one thing that might be helpful."

"What is it, Harry?" I replied.

"Well, Don, I noticed that you're standing too close to the ball after you hit it," was his sage advice.

Another time, I was golfing in Leduc with my brother-in-law, Al Peter. One of his friends was an eighty-some-year-old ex-pilot. I was having a terrible time, and finally this eighty-some-year-old stepped in.

"Don," he said, "let me see your club."

He then stood beside the ball, took a swing, and hit the ball 150 or 200 yards straight down the fairway.

He handed me back my club with the observation, "It's not the club."

I still enjoy golfing and get out a couple of times each week. God impressed on me years ago that this is a game, not how I make my living. I'm out here for the exercise and to enjoy nature with friends. The main feature of my golf game is that I am very good at finding golf balls that other people have abandoned. In a sense, not too much has changed since my childhood when my talent was finding money outside the dance hall!

19. Spiritual Life

It is important at this stage to reflect on what was happening in my life besides my professional development. When I look at my Christian character formation, the church and the culture of the church certainly played a significant role in my development. I have listened to many sermons, and while this definitely played a part in forming my spiritual values, much of my discipling occurred outside of the church programs.

Amazing things were happening in Western Canada during this time. In 1971, revival broke out in Saskatoon, Saskatchewan, at a little church called Ebenezer Baptist after some evangelistic meetings where the Sutera Twins preached. There was widespread repentance resulting in community transformation as people confessed to all manner of sins and made restitution for their wrongdoing.

A team of people came to our church in Edmonton from Saskatoon to share what God had been doing, and Gerry's sister, Ardice, was part of this group. As they shared, I was convicted that while I could defend my faith if someone asked me questions, I did not have a freedom to share Jesus in a personal way with those I met on a daily basis. The Spirit of God was moving, and I found myself kneeling and weeping before God for two hours while He brought transformation to my heart. Even now as I recall that time, I am brought to tears by the powerful sense of God's presence and work in my life.

After that time, there was a definite freedom and courage that allowed me to speak joyfully about Jesus. Talking about what God was teaching me and sharing scripture became a natural, spontaneous part of my interactions with people. This new freedom from fear was also a factor in allowing me to take the step of moving from the security of my job at the hospital into the uncertainty of a home care startup.

One occasion I recall involved a patient at the Royal Alex who was going to need respiratory care after leaving the hospital. I listened to the patient talk about his concerns and then talked about the home care service we could provide. I ended by singing a little blessing to the patient, not realizing that the call system was on and that my little song was being broadcast to the nursing station as well. This did not become an issue of contention, but it was a reflection of the changes that had occurred in this caregiver's heart.

The revival that began in Saskatoon was the start of a discipling pattern in my life. The discipleship movement and the charismatic renewal or charismatic movement were probably the most profound factors in bringing change and renewal to my life. I came in contact with a group of leaders who were published in a magazine called New Wine. They were also providing teaching ministries and sermons which had a tremendous effect on my personal spiritual growth.

When I look at the titles and denominations used to describe different expressions of faith in churches today, I'm not easily put into one box. When people ask me what I am, I have found that the best answer is "I am a sinner being rescued by Jesus, just like you!" If pressed for a label, I reply that I am an "ecumeniac" (picture an ecumenical who is crazy about Jesus). My spiritual journey has been influenced by a number of streams of Christian practice. My spiritual birth and current faith situation would put me in the category of being charismatic or Pentecostal. My church affiliation has been primarily Baptist. My exposure to many Catholics has had a deep influence on my faith, and being involved with many para-church organizations has widened my theological perspectives. I have also read extensively from many of these areas.

I believe in the church. I believe in its mission. However, the Western church and the current practice of many churches are in conflict with the culture in which we live. As God has moved my vocational life and my social life away from the programs of the church, I have found a ministry of sharing Jesus that has caused me to have less time for church programs and more time for living in the community. It could be said that I'm realizing faith doesn't have as much to do with church attendance as it does with loving people.

During this time of caring for people in the hospital, there are a few stories that I feel a need to share that display the change occurring within me as I interacted with these people who were in our intensive care unit.

There was a wonderful young woman who found herself in intensive care after a serious accident. She had been hitchhiking and got a ride with someone who attempted to molest her. She jumped out of the vehicle to get away and sustained serious injuries, including broken hips and smashed up legs. She was the first person that we placed on a volume ventilator. She had chest tubes coming out of her, but she was mentally fit while we were caring for her. There was a connection, and I felt like she trusted me.

She acquired Klebsiella pneumonia from bacteria that probably came from somewhere in the bowel. Due to her weakened respiratory system, the bacteria caused a severe infection. When she went to the OR to have surgery, she could not be without 100 percent oxygen, and so nitrous oxide was not an option to sedate her. She woke up during surgery and required open chest cardiac massage to get her heart beating again. She survived that surgery but succumbed to disease a few days later. Losing a young person like that had a profound impact on me and impressed upon me the realization that God was present and every opportunity to interact with a person was ministry whether we spoke of Jesus or not.

One day, an elderly Romanian lady came into my office at the hospital. She sat in the chair next to my desk and in broken English told me that her husband was in intensive care and not expected to live. He was in his seventies with a combination of cardiac and pulmonary conditions, and had suffered a cardiac arrest while shoveling his walk. He had been brought into the hospital and placed on a ventilator. I reached across the desk to take this woman's hand, and we prayed for her husband. When I went to the ICU to see this man, it was obvious that he was not in good shape and that it would take a miracle for him to recover. The next day, he came out of his coma, and within a few days, he was weaned off the ventilator.

Would you believe that this man became one of the people we provided with oxygen home care? When he was discharged and I went to their home to set him up on the oxygen equipment, the family was celebrating his recovery and offered me wine in fine European custom. I declined the offer saying that I didn't drink alcohol. They then offered coffee which I accepted, but it was so strong it made my heart beat nearly out of my chest! Perhaps I should have gone with the wine!

They became favourite patients of our home care business, and our drivers loved to deliver oxygen to them. The drivers always left their home with a big bag of cookies and a smile, feeling not only appreciated but like part of the family. You never knew what you would encounter when you went to see this patient; he might be up repairing his roof or busy with another household project. He had a hard time limiting his activities to match his cardiac respiratory condition. It was a joy to see him living life to the full, and I marvelled at how well they treated us.

On one occasion, my visit to them coincided with the mailman's arrival, and I discovered that they treated him with the same love and appreciation they did our team. They were such lovely genuine people, and I loved experiencing the hospitality of their culture.

In time, John succumbed to his illness, and the family asked one of the drivers and me to be pallbearers for his funeral. We had never experienced a service like that before. I think they were Catholic or Orthodox, and as we sat in the front row, his widow almost crawled into the coffin with her husband, so overcome with grief that I thought for sure we would have to support her and the family afterwards with counselors and ministry.

However, after the burial, we discovered that the church took over all these things and was very good at supporting this family as they processed their grief. This woman obviously missed her husband, but she just had a more overt way of expressing grief in her culture than we were accustomed to. These patients and others were used by God during this season to teach me how to serve, how to support, and how to be part of the journey of others in many different ways.

20. Career Development

At this stage in our profession, there were opportunities to go almost anywhere that you wanted if you were ready. Because I had American registration, and one of my former colleagues as a student was in the United States, there was opportunity to consider a career move south of the border. Our involvement in publishing the respiratory journal also resulted in a lot of contacts.

One of these was with a hospital in Pittsburgh where Jim Whitaker, who was high up in the respiratory profession, was the manager of the department. I applied to work in this hospital, and they had accepted me to go down and work with Jim. I might have ended up as a Pittsburgh Penguins fan; however, the hospital was unable to get a green card for me to work in the United States.

About that time, the Foothills hospital in Calgary was being built, and one of the people who was part of the medical staff at the Royal Alex, Dr. Fred Parny, had accepted a position to oversee anaesthesia at the new hospital. He liked what he saw in me and invited me to his home to be interviewed. He offered me the position of head of respiratory at the Foothills, and I had accepted that position, even going down to Calgary to interview. However, my boss at the Royal Alex accepted a position at the Cook County hospital in Chicago, and the Royal Alex asked me to stay on as the director of respiratory. I cancelled my plans to go to Calgary and stayed on at the Royal Alex, continuing my development there.

Don Smailes (seated) and Lorne White at Royal Alex Hospital

My first assistant was Colin Wallace Tarry, and we had a wonderful working relationship, even though it didn't last for as long as we may have planned. Colin and his wife Carol decided that they wanted to go back to Ontario, and Colin became the person who introduced respiratory into both North Bay hospitals where they lived.

When I reflect on the number of people who were trained at the Royal Alex, and the leadership positions they graduated to, the number is absolutely astounding. Mac Scott and Nick Papp went down to a hospital in Lethbridge, Tom Annable and Murray Yarish both developed the department in the Red Deer hospital, and Ram Prasad went up to Grande Prairie. They were all graduates of the program at the Royal Alex, and it enriches my life to see how many people came through and made a difference in so many areas. It was a wonderful time to be involved in the formation of a profession.

Your formation always takes years, and there are people who make greater than average contributions to that development. In my journey, Klaus Becker would be one of those people, and perhaps the person who affected me the most would be Dr. Chris Varvis.

Dr. Varvis was the medical director of our respiratory program at the Royal Alex. His background as an internist and respirologist made him an amazing teacher. When he taught pulmonary physiology, he drew pictures and was able to explain complex things in a way that we could grasp. When he was doing rounds, he took us with him and allowed us to listen to chests. As we heard different breath sounds, he told us what we were hearing.

I will never forget Dr. Varvis calling us to the bedside of a patient who was the oldest person with the most advanced case of cystic fibrosis the hospital had seen. He was in his twenties, but you almost never saw anyone who survived cystic fibrosis much longer than childhood. However, through advances in the treatment of respiratory disease, we got to meet this amazing person who was a true survivor in every sense of the word.

Dr. Varvis's influence was not confined to the clinical setting. When we graduated, he took us along with our spouses to the Steak Loft to celebrate. This was my first exposure to a restaurant where Caesar salads were prepared at the table while we watched. Dr. Varvis also hosted numerous suppers at the University of Alberta faculty club where there were various wines between the many courses of the meal. He was incredibly gracious and unaffected as he shared his enjoyment of "the finer things" with us, and he never treated us as less than equals, even though we were quite naïve when it came to "high society."

My only golf game at the Derrick country club was also a result of his generosity. In addition, I cherished his wise counsel when we ventured into the home care business and experienced the challenges of dealing with government bureaucracy.

Dr. Varvis ordered many of the respiratory treatments we supplied for his patients. One machine that we had was called a coughlater. The coughlater had a mask attachment and would use positive pressure to inflate the lungs, then quickly switch to negative pressure to simulate a cough which would help dislodge mucous from the chest. We tried this and other therapies on ourselves before performing them on patients, which was a good way to develop empathy.

It was an interesting teaching technique, especially when it came to learning things like arterial punctures and deep suctioning. Attempting deep suctioning on yourself is a challenging process; you soon find that inserting the suction tube into your nose and easing it down into your lungs is not a pleasant experience. Lubricating the end of the tube certainly helps, but having that experience of tearing up when the suction tube passes through the upper nasal passages and irritates the mucous membranes makes you much more compassionate when you have to perform the procedure on patients.

For many procedures, it also means that you are motivated to try different ways of doing things to make necessary interventions less uncomfortable. Dr. Varvis became a patient at the Royal Alex on one occasion. He ordered a coughlater treatment for himself after surgery, since this was one therapy he routinely ordered for his post operative patients. After experiencing one treatment, he was convinced never to order it for another patient. I think that if you find any coughlaters today, they would be relics and examples of equipment that didn't quite make it to the marketplace since their efficacy was overshadowed by how unpleasant they were for patients.

As our respiratory department continued to thrive and word got out about us, we had many visitors. Dr. Varvis became the head of the Canadian Medical Society, and their convention came to Edmonton. As we went about our tasks in the hospital, we were interviewed as part of the presentation to the conference attendees.

I remember speaking in the ICU about how we sterilized equipment using a cold sterilization technique with Cidex. It was very effective at killing any bacteria and was much easier on the plastic components of our machines, like tubing, masks, and so forth. After I finished speaking, I went off to continue with my work, not realizing that there was to be a question-and-answer period about our use of Cidex glutaraldehyde. I was in the respiratory cleaning area washing pediatric croup canopies when I should have been answering questions. That was embarrassing, but it was also a reflection of the variety of our assigned tasks in respiratory. We were certainly never bored since there was always something to do, and it was a very fulfilling career.

We also had the opportunity to be pioneers with new medications. We got to talk to pharmaceutical representatives about the various medications and how we applied them, as well as what the results were. We had opportunities to give lectures and demonstrations, and then we got to play golf with the reps. Because we were pioneers in the respiratory area, we became somewhat notorious. Those were very pleasant memories and very often developmental experiences.

One of the stories I love to tell about Dr. Varvis occurred when we were doing medical rounds with him one day. For some reason, we had X-rays up on the screen, and Dr. Varvis made the comment while looking at the images, "This is like trying to make chicken soup out of chicken shit." I was called to the front of the group and was asked about something. As I spoke, I didn't realize that my fly was open. I wasn't trying to be an exhibitionist, but someone brought it to my attention, causing me some embarrassment as I quickly zipped up. Dr. Varvis got up and said, "Oh Don, you don't have to worry about that. Dead birds never fall out of the nest." That was one of the greatest responses to an embarrassing situation and I often wish I could remember to use it.

My time at the Royal Alex treating patients coincided with a family emergency involving my sister Phyllis and her husband. Phyllis had been working as a nurse in a mission in the Northwest Territories when she met and fell in love with a fisherman named Fred McCordic. They married and had two wonderful sons, Rick and Jim.

They were raising their family when Fred became sick and was brought to Edmonton for treatment. At the Royal Alex, they discovered that he had a primary cancer of the liver. This is very rare, since the liver is usually a secondary site of a cancer that has spread, and it can be disastrous. For whatever reason, this happened, and there was no viable treatment or cure for the cancer. Fred had also developed pneumonia, and his physicians had decided that it would be foolish to treat the pneumonia aggressively since the liver cancer made his condition terminal.

What the physicians didn't know was that Fred and Phyllis were trying to resolve some issues in their marriage and in their family, and they needed time to devote to this. They were also people of faith who believed God could heal Fred, and they were trusting Him to work in their lives.

When I read Fred's chart, I discovered that the decision had been made not to treat the pneumonia, and I challenged that decision saying, "No, he must be treated."

The director of medical students discovered that I had been looking in this patient's chart, and he reported me to my administrative director, Dr. M. I found myself in his office, having to explain why I had looked at this chart and why I had intervened. As a respiratory therapist, I had access to patient charts, but Dr. G objected to my interference in the decision that had been made regarding the patient's treatment.

I explained the extenuating circumstances in the life of this patient that I was privy to because he and his wife were family members, and

Dr. M understood and supported my position. Fred was treated for his pneumonia, and while it didn't change the ultimate outcome of the disease process, it did give him and Phyllis the extra time they needed to focus on their relationship and their family.

This experience was another instance where I learned the privilege and responsibility that accompany being a part of the treatment team. It was a helpful lesson in how to converse with physicians and how to listen to patients to ensure that healthcare decisions are not made solely based on practical considerations of mortality and disease processes.

Allowing the Spirit of God to guide me into a place of truly hearing what patients are saying and looking at how to care for and support them has been something I aspire to. It has been a learning process to develop the ability to listen and then communicate with the healthcare team.

In respiratory, the things that we do for patients are always initiated by a physician's order. We don't practice medicine; we implement our treatments and therapy according to what the doctor has ordered. Learning to listen to the patients and really hear their needs, however, can help us tailor what has been prescribed by the physician to make sure it does the most good.

I have been blessed with a wonderful body. It's not much to look at and doesn't always perform the way I want it to, yet I have experienced a very good record of health overall. I have some allergies and am prone to sinus infections, but I've learned to fight these before they move down into my lungs and cause more serious problems. During my eighteen years at the Royal Alexandra Hospital, I only had a couple of serious health issues. One was the blood poisoning episode which has already been recounted.

The second illness was when I contracted pneumonia while working in respiratory. I was sent home for a week, and Dr. Varvis prescribed mustard plasters and antibiotics. Sweating from the mustard plasters and coughing up all the junk in my lungs was no fun, but the treatments worked, and soon I was fine.

The health plan at the Royal Alex was such that each month, you were allowed a certain number of sick days for which you were paid. My good health meant that when I left the Royal Alex after eighteen years, there was sick pay added to my final paycheque, which was helpful when we embarked on the adventure of home care.

During this time at the hospital, we had an outpatient department where patients would come to the hospital to receive intermittent positive pressure breathing (IPPB) treatments. We also administered misted bronchodilators and humidified air to try to liquefy the bronchial secretions and clear the airways of affected patients.

The phenomena of a hyperactive airway, and the distress and danger it presents to the sufferer, is probably not fully appreciated by anyone who hasn't experienced it. An asthma attack—or narrowing of the airway because it becomes plugged with secretions—makes the work of breathing more difficult than shovelling heavy snow at full speed. All the energy that the body can produce is used up just by breathing.

In the early days of respiratory, that was one of the main treatments sought, and people would come into the hospital for relief. From this, there evolved home care businesses that respiratory therapists got involved in as they made equipment available. The hospital would refer patients to get those treatments on a regular basis. This system carried on for several years, but it became obvious that changes were needed.

The problem with having the patients come to the hospital for treatment, especially in our Canadian winters, was that while the patients would get some benefit from the treatment, by the time they travelled home, they were often in distress again. The hospital had funding for outpatient treatments, but not for home care. In 1969, we had an experience that brought things to a head.

We had referred a patient to a home-care company, and the patient had purchased some equipment for about four hundred dollars. The patient had one or two treatments, but within days, succumbed to an infection that took their life. After the patient passed away, the family was offered one hundred dollars for essentially new equipment by the home care business.

It so happened that this patient was a friend of the administrator of the Royal Alex Hospital, Mr. Nye. I heard about this directly from the irate administrator who asked why we were referring people to this kind of business. I replied, "Mr. Nye, now you know why the hospital should be in this business."

He made a statement that ended up changing my life: "The hospital can't do it, but you can."

That started a home care service that became Alberta Respiratory Services Associates Ltd. This was in November of 1969. Letters of incorporation were filed, and four strapping young respiratory therapists began a new venture that changed my life.

The original partners were Don Smailes, Lorne White, Nelson Kennedy, and Henry Van Reede. All of us were involved in the Royal Alex, although it's possible that at that time Nelson had already moved; however, I think he was still a part of our team. We later added another shareholder, Bob Wilkie, who was to come in.

Since we were still employed at the hospital and did not need to make a living, we set up a little organization where we could acquire equipment from the manufacturers. We would sell it to the patients and teach them how to use it. When they no longer needed it, we would take it back and clean it up for someone else to use. This was something we could do after hours and on weekends, and we did not need to earn a salary from this work; we were simply responding to an immediate need. It eventually did become a living, but that will be discussed more in a later chapter.

21. What Is Family For?

The early 1970s brought a new experience to my life. Somehow, I received word that Lorna, my stepmother, was experiencing pathological fractures in her legs as a result of metastatic breast cancer. Her sister Rose, who was also her best friend and a great help to her while living in Prince Albert, made us aware that Dad was not working, and the family was in dire need of assistance. I decided that I could help, and we moved the family to Edmonton.

We found a little house for them on 120th Street just north of Jasper Avenue, near the Allen Clinic. Jackie, the youngest family member, was about six years old, and Mark, Tim, Brent, and Graham were also living at home and relocated to Edmonton. Laurie was married and established in The Pas, Manitoba. Gail was married and had a home in Saskatoon. Carol was finishing school, and I'm not sure of her living circumstances at that time.

God provided a wonderful physician by the name of Dr. Penny at the Allen Clinic who helped Lorna face the challenge of a non-treatable cancer. My brother Jerry and his wife Donna responded to the need and also became involved in helping the family. I was able to find a job for Dad working in housekeeping at the Royal Alex since I was still working there in respiratory.

As Lorna faced this terminal illness, her main concern was that her children be cared for after her death. She had come to the realization that Dad's life was not going to change and that he would be unable to care for their children.

On Halloween, Lorna and the kids came over, and while the children went trick-or-treating in our neighbourhood, Lorna and I had a prayer meeting. There were many tears as she planned for the care of her family and faced her impending mortality. She wanted to go back to Saskatchewan, and arrangements were made for the future of her children.

My brother Jerry decided, with Lorna's approval, to adopt Mark and Tim into his family legally so that he could raise them as his own. Jackie went to live with her sister, Gail, and Brent went to live with a cousin, Karen, and her husband. Graham went to live on a ranch in southern

Saskatchewan for a time, and Jerry coordinated with family there for his care.

When these plans were put in place, Lorna moved back to Saskatchewan, and the children went to their new homes. Dad continued to work at the Royal Alex and came to live in our home. This caused a great deal of stress in our household since his lifestyle was totally unacceptable to my wife, Gerry. I faced the difficult task of telling my father that he could no longer live with us.

It came to light that he was also lying to his employers at the Royal Alex about his work absences when he was going back and forth to Saskatchewan. I told the hospital that I believed they should terminate his employment because he was not being truthful.

Lorna faced her final days bravely and was laid to rest in the Prince Albert cemetery near her mother. These experiences during Lorna's illness created a bond between me and my stepmother that totally overshadowed any struggles we had when she first entered our family during my childhood. I have fond memories of this brave woman who faced an impossible situation and was able to leave this earth in peace, knowing that her children were cared for.

Dad's life disintegrated even further as his alcoholism progressed, and he ended up living on the streets. My sisters would call to tell me about his situation. Eventually, he had a stroke and ended up in a nursing home in Saskatoon. I visited him during this time, and he came out to Gail's home for supper one evening.

He had difficulty swallowing and lost his temper, taking out his frustration on those around him. I took control of the situation, informing him that his behaviour was unacceptable, and he went back to the care facility. I don't know how long it was before he succumbed to respiratory and cardiac complications, but I do remember his funeral in Prince Albert.

The Pentecostal pastor graciously performed the service for Dad, and I gave a tribute, talking about what I had learned from him. Much of what I had learned, I learned from his failures, and I am so grateful to God for the transforming power of faith in Jesus that allowed me to live a different life than he did. I did not learn much about fathering from my father, but I have forgiven him for his shortcomings and how they affected my life. I am thankful for the other examples in the community that taught me how to be a good man, husband, and father. The second family also survived the scars of their lives and have grown into people who would make their mother proud.

Smailes siblings gathered after Jack Smailes' funeral. Back row L–R: Mark, Tim, Brent, Graham, Don, Jerry. Middle L–R: Laurie, Pat, Jackie, Gail, Lynn. Front L–R: friend, Phyllis, Carol.

22. The ARS Story

A new business needs a name, so we became Alberta Respiratory Services Associates Limited. Not the catchiest name for a new venture, but it made sense with the service we sought to provide, our location, and the fact that there were four of us. We weren't aiming to build a successful business; we were simply responding to a need and seeking to solve a problem. Although there was oxygen home care available in Alberta at the time, the existing company was not meeting the needs of the customers.

Lorne White, Henry van Reede, Nelson Kennedy, and I were the original four people to share this concern, and we decided to do something about it. Nelson had connections in the legal realm, and we incorporated. The cost of incorporation was $360, so we all threw some cash into the "hat" to pay for it. We never really intended to make money with this new enterprise; it was a response to a need in the community. With permission from the hospital, we were able to begin.

Our referral source came quite naturally from the people we were treating in the hospital or from patients of the physicians we served. The equipment and treatment most commonly ordered was either intermittent positive pressure breathing or aerosol therapy where compressors and nebulizers delivered medication to patients. At that time, most people who needed supplemental oxygen were admitted to healthcare institutions and became patients. Oxygen in the home was still very rare, but there was definitely a need for it.

When someone needed home oxygen therapy, we would provide the initial equipment including regulators, tubing, and nasal cannula or mask. We would then refer them to an oxygen supplier in the area, generally the same companies who manufactured oxygen for welders. We did the initial set-up, patient teaching, and training in how to use the therapy successfully, and then we never dealt with those patients again unless there was a problem.

The limited number of patients we were seeing allowed us to do this after hours and on weekends. Because my role at the hospital consisted of mostly administration, I relished the opportunity to do patient care and did most of the actual patient set-up and teaching.

Our full-time employment at the hospital, and corresponding income, meant it was not necessary for the business to make money. At the end of the year, we usually had a surplus of a few thousand dollars that was divided amongst the shareholders.

We knew respiratory people all over Alberta, and it became a pattern that we would provide the equipment to the respiratory therapists in the community, paying them to do the initial patient set-up. This enabled the doctors' orders to be carried out without requiring us to travel long distances, and the patients were looked after. Word got out that this service was available, and that was how the business grew. Physicians from all over Alberta would refer patients from different communities with respiratory needs, and we responded by meeting those needs.

By the year 1975, it became obvious that we could not continue to meet these needs with only part-time therapists, so we hired Ralph Sperry, a recent graduate of the respiratory program at NAIT as our first full-time respiratory therapist (RT).

Ralph Sperry, the first full-time employee of ARS

It's interesting to reflect on the little things that became big things. We needed a logo to put on the patient training and informational material we were producing at this time. We wanted something to symbolize our business.

An artist who worked for the secretarial company of our former landlady, Betty, came up with a logo depicting a house with an oxygen cylinder. We decided on red ink simply because that was my favourite colour. I'm sure a lot more planning and research would go into developing a brand today, but that logo served us well for many years.

The beginning of a business responding to the needs in the community was a new adventure. This undertaking continued for some nine years before sparking a major change in my own vocation.

In the beginning, I had no intention of changing my lifestyle, so for nine years I continued looking after patients in their homes while still working full time at the Royal Alex as director of respiratory. However, in hindsight it is obvious that what I learned at the hospital was valuable training for what the business would later require.

The respiratory department at the Royal Alex continued to grow. The addition of intensive care medicine and neonatal care at that site progressed with physicians that were trained and passionate about these fields. This caused our scope of practice to change significantly.

We went from primarily looking after people with chronic lung disease conditions generally associated with aging and lifestyle, to caring for patients with complications from surgery and accidents that required respiratory support.

As a department head, I was learning how to be a manager and experiencing all the challenges that accompany that role. From motivating people, to responding to government edicts; learning how to cooperate with other departments and performing all the tasks associated with administration. I was being stretched in areas I never dreamed existed in concert with patient care.

A great blessing at this time was building a friendship with a colleague who worked in physiotherapy and lived in the same neighbourhood as we did. We would carpool to work, and while talking about the similar administrative duties we had, I gleaned a great deal from his expertise. Learning how to prepare budgets and operate within them, how to hire staff and deal with personnel issues, how to negotiate with government agencies who were needing to control the costs of healthcare, while seeing the people who were trying to deliver healthcare and facing the need for staff and supplies. All of these issues became the major focus of my work, and, while rising to meet the challenges and solve these problems brought a measure of satisfaction, it didn't bring the same fulfillment I had when caring for patients. In retrospect, this is probably why I did most of the after-hours home care for our fledgling business. I needed to feel appreciated on a personal level, and the interaction involved in meeting the immediate needs of a patient in their home provided that.

Understanding how to build a team was a huge part of what was cultivated in me as I learned how to lead a department. Developing people in the profession of respiratory therapy added value to the department and the hospital as a whole. Even though the administration was not as gratifying to me as the more immediate rewards of patient care, I can see that God was preparing me with necessary skills for the next phase of His plan for my life.

The security that comes from your value in your profession is one thing, but the satisfaction that you get from what you do can become a competing factor in decision-making as it pertains to your career. With the growth of our home care business, it became evident that ARS needed more attention than what just one full-time employee could give. I began to feel that God might be moving me towards embracing home care full time.

How does one move from what might be perceived as the peak of your career development into something that might not even pay the bills? I found myself wrestling with this idea and trying to peer into the future to see if I could make a living in home care, or whether the risk of failure was too great. I spoke with the other partners in ARS and the hospital administration as I moved towards a decision.

Although I was willing to take the risk of seeing if I could make a go of full-time home care, I wasn't willing to take the risk of ruining the investments already made by the other original shareholders. I asked if they would be willing to sell their shares to me, and I think we paid two thousand dollars per shareholder. Then we reorganized the company so that the shareholders were my wife and me; I held 51 percent of the shares and Gerry held 49 percent.

23. Transitions

The decision to transfer from the security of a position in the hospital to the risk of making a living in home care was not made lightly. I had come to the realization that I enjoyed patient care much more than the administrative duties that characterized much of my role leading the respiratory department at the hospital. There was certainly a need for respiratory home care in the community, but the question was whether a home care startup could earn enough to cover the real costs of equipment as well as provide a wage sufficient to support a family.

With some counsel from trusted friends and colleagues, and much prayer, the decision to strike out on this new adventure was made. My departure from the hospital allowed colleagues who were ready and able to move up and take over the tasks I was leaving.

Since the ability to make a living and provide for my family in home care was still uncertain, I made an arrangement with the hospital. If within six months I realized that the home care business was not sufficient to support my family, I could return to the hospital as a general duty RT. This allowed me to try something that I sensed God wanted me to do, while still having some security that I would have a job if we were not successful with ARS.

The challenges of funding a new business soon became evident, and it was almost overwhelming for this farm boy from Saskatchewan. We had to learn to navigate the government oxygen programs to pay for equipment and services for our patients. However, this didn't cover the start-up costs of acquiring the apparatus and oxygen to begin with. I had to arrange bankers for the business, and we placed our home as collateral to finance the risks of beginning this venture.

The stresses on my wife Gerry and her support of this change were remarkable. Our home became the headquarters of the business, resulting in oxygen paraphernalia everywhere. My children remember a notebook by the phone to take messages from patients needing service calls, as well as washing equipment in the kitchen sink.

Problem-solving in a new vocation and location was not new. The experiences of developing a profession in the hospital had been God's preparation for this new challenge. Ralph Sperry had become our first full-time employee in 1975, and in 1978 when I left the hospital, I joined him in full-time home care work. There was no guaranteed pension or salary, but I was at peace, knowing that God had His hand on my life and was directing my steps.

Because we had very few patients to begin with, we did not even have an oxygen supply system set up. When an oxygen patient was generated through a referral from the hospital or physician, we would go with our automobiles to the oxygen depot to pick up what we needed. We were not familiar with Canadian Liquid Air's standards of safety. We were young people with energy, and we knew what our patients needed. There was a large room with the available cylinders which were familiar to us. We had no trucks to haul the tanks, so we managed with what we did have.

Oxygen comes in cylinders in a variety of sizes. Portables were labelled as "D" and "E" tanks, and had fifteen or twenty-six cubic feet of oxygen compressed to twenty-three hundred pounds per square inch. Larger "H" cylinders had 244 cubic feet of oxygen and weighed about 150 pounds each. To contain this kind of pressure, cylinders were made of high-quality steel, and the oxygen supplier had many of these cylinders in stock.

Providing a patient with oxygen that would last two or three days meant we required large H cylinders. We would come to the depot, take the necessary cylinders, and put them in our cars to take to the patients. This violated most of the rules that the oxygen depot had for handling oxygen tanks. We had no trucks to transport the small amounts of oxygen we were using, so we made do with our personal vehicles and muscle power.

I remember carrying one of these big cylinders on my shoulder up the stairs of a three-storey apartment and securing it in the patient's residence. I like to joke that I was once six feet tall, but that carrying 150-pound oxygen tanks on my shoulders for years reduced my height to its current measure of 5'6".

In the early days, I remember delivering oxygen to a patient in the countryside and calculating the cost of the cylinder, how much we could charge the patient or home care program for it, and then figuring out how many cylinders I would need in order to pay myself a certain rate per month.

It was not always possible to park right next to the home of a patient to deliver oxygen, and in wintertime, this could be especially problematic. One instance stands out in my memory when we had to park in an alley, load the heavy oxygen cylinder onto a little cart, and drag it about a block over snowbanks to get to the patient's door. By the time we had done this three times to deliver the necessary tanks, our little oxygen transport cart was totally destroyed. That led us to find someone who could build a better cart to withstand the rigours of regular use in unpredictable conditions.

As we progressed to having more oxygen patients, we secured used trucks that we modified to hold the oxygen cylinders upright. A delivery driver was soon added to our team as well.

Richard Zimmerman delivers oxygen to a client

We didn't have any lifts on the back of our trucks, so we would move the cylinder to the back of the truck and drop it the two or three feet to the pavement below. When moving the cylinder from truck to pavement, we would hold on to the metal cap on top of the cylinder. Depending on how new the cylinder was, the top was often not held securely by the threads and would come off in your hand.

When a 150-pound weight is suddenly released, that cap comes off with some force that can result in a knockout punch to the jaw. I believe every one of us got smacked in the face with the steel top of the cylinder, and we soon learned there had to be a better way to make sure that any errant cylinder parts went past your ear or beside your head rather than to your jaw. We never realized delivering oxygen cylinders could be training for ducking and weaving in boxing! We learned how to handle these things by working with them, not unlike the trial and error involved in other learning experiences.

Handling of steel products that are highly pressurized demands respect for the contents. A steel cylinder that is pressurized with gas of twenty-two hundred square pounds per square inch becomes a dangerous weapon if the valve is knocked off. When the gas is suddenly released, the cylinder becomes a missile, demolishing anything in its path until the gas is depleted. We taught our patients these kind of safety things, but we did not always practice what we preached in terms of cylinder safety.

We had heard of incidents where a cylinder fell from the delivery truck, breaking off its valve and flying across the road like an errant torpedo. Thankfully this never happened to any of our workers, but we were cognizant of the risks and the damage that could result from this sort of incident. Dealing with oxygen tanks requires caution, and it is not something one should attempt without a healthy respect for pressurized gas.

How do you compete with welding distributors when it comes to getting cylinders from the dock of Canadian Liquid Air? These were always the priority customers, and after waiting to be served with the cylinders we needed while being ignored and passed over in favour of the bigger volume welding customers, I would simply go and get the oxygen myself, bring it to the dock, and load it in my truck. That got us in some trouble, but I remember saying to the Canadian Liquid Air people, "One day, we will be your largest distributor!" I had no idea at that time of how prophetic my statement would be.

We managed through these difficult times and our oxygen business grew. As we tried to solve some of our oxygen supply problems, we considered changing suppliers. However, we realized that a new supplier would not necessarily mean better service since home oxygen was still a small part of the demand in the aerosol gas business. As we examined the oxygen supply agreement we had with CLA, we further discovered that it could easily be interpreted as an acquisition agreement. The contracts with oxygen manufacturers were structured in such a way that if we ever went out of business, and I was not personally in charge, the oxygen company would be given first right of refusal to buy the company.

As we sought to improve this situation, we realized that the best solution would be to sell part of our business to the supplier. We eventually sold 35 percent of our business to CLA and saw a definite improvement in service when they became shareholders, and had a seat on the board.

Around this time, the government of Alberta got involved in developing oxygen concentrators that would separate air into oxygen and nitrogen in patients' homes. We were aware of this, and the government had invested significant money into these devices. The government had about thirty-five patients who were outfitted with these machines, and we took over these patients, committing to look after them.

The problem was that the engineers designing these concentrators were constantly attempting to improve them, with the result that the machines often did not work in the patient's home. We made an offer to the government oxygen program, proposing that we would look after these patients and provide the concentrators. We found a concentrator that worked very well, and that contract with the government became a way of funding our home care business.

24. Building the ARS Team

In 1978 or 1979, shortly after I had left the Royal Alex hospital to join Ralph in working full time in our home care business, things began to change. Ralph and I were quite happy to work from home with half of our equipment at his place and half at mine.

The ARS story is really a story of teambuilding. The accomplishments of this business were a result of the people who were a part of the team. As I reflect on this amazing group of people, I see God's hand in providing the necessary human resources before we even realized what was being built as a business. It is often the case: credit for the accomplishments of an organization often goes to the leaders, while the real success comes from the efforts of the team.

As mentioned before, we were not seeking to build a business when ARS began; we were simply responding to a need. I believe God was working behind the scenes as He often does, to do much more than we could imagine. ARS did not belong to Don and Gerry Smailes; it belonged to God, and I saw myself as His instrument to effect change in the world.

In the same way, the ARS team was not handpicked by me, but God, in His providence, put the right people in our path and brought together an amazing group of individuals to build a home care business.

Ralph Sperry was our first employee, as mentioned earlier. As the business began to grow, God brought to my attention an amazing woman by the name of Caroline Zeitner. She was the widow of one of my best friends and was raising four incredible sons. She agreed to take on the responsibility of billing the government for our respiratory home care business. She rearranged her home to make an office in one of the bedrooms. We would drop off the paperwork for what we had provided to patients while she did the rest.

The government of Alberta had a program called Alberta Aids to Daily Living (AADL) that helped with the cost of oxygen and other respiratory equipment needed to support patients at home. Caroline learned to navigate the program, determining which of our patients were eligible and applying on their behalf to have the home care costs covered. This was how we as a company were paid by the government for our work. Learning the AADL billing system, keeping track of our patient billing files, and all of the ins and outs of the program fell under Caroline's responsibility. She rose to the challenge admirably.

As the business grew, we recruited more people to help Caroline with billing including Elli Zapf and Ellen Breitkreuz. This amazing team navigated the red tape of government billing with excellence and integrity. We didn't have to train them; rather, they would tell us what was needed to qualify for funding. Their faith and Christ-like character were reflected in their work ethic and the way they interacted with patients, government agencies, and other employees. They were respected and beloved by all.

When we had a patient on oxygen therapy, we would bill the government for a month's rental of the oxygen concentrator along with the care we provided. If the patient's services were discontinued because of death, a move out of province, or some other circumstances, we would refund the unused portion of the charges back to the government. When we did this, Mrs. T, our contact at AADL, would have to figure out how to credit the program for what had been paid. We got the impression that this had not happened before, but we believed that we should not charge the program for services that had not been provided. This honest approach was one reason that even those who received invoices from the ladies in our billing department held them in such high esteem.

The business grew much faster than I had ever anticipated, and we soon had to face the reality that our vans and homes were insufficient to house the equipment we needed to supply for our patients. There was equipment everywhere, and often Gerry couldn't see the living room floor beneath all of the home care supplies that had spilled over out of the bedroom originally designated as the ARS office.

Since our economic situation was also improving with the growth of the business, we began to search for a new home. We found a great place at 18024 84th Avenue that had lots of room and space to build a garage. Our thought was that we could build the garage and driveway to accommodate the growing needs of our business. Little did we know that by the time we got the garage built and moved the home care equipment in, the business would have outgrown even that space.

We found a warehouse located at 117th Avenue to rent. Our wonderful friend Dan Reese, a talented builder, was able to convert the space into the perfect combination of offices, repair shop, and storage for our needs. The warehouses on either side were occupied by a furniture manufacturer and an engineer in the oil business. At Christmas, an organization selling business gifts recommended for companies to give to their customers came to the various establishments in our neighbourhood. I remember feeling the pressure to purchase something for our clients like the engineer next door did, but we simply didn't have the finances to do that.

A few years later, we bought the warehouse from this engineer to expand ARS while the engineer found himself looking for work elsewhere due to changes in the oil industry. This was just another indication of how God led us to do the work, simply and without fanfare, and how we were able to grow as a result.

Some of the most important people in our business were those who delivered oxygen to our patients. We called them truck drivers, but they were really so much more. They were front line representatives of the company and an integral part of the ARS team.

It so happened that my brother Brent needed a job when we were looking for drivers, and he became a wonderful part of the business. He was not hired because he was my brother; he was God's gift to us when we needed a driver and he needed a job. As a hard-working, tough, yet friendly individual, Brent was a favourite with those he served as well as those he worked with. His work ethic and sense of humour came in handy when he had to deliver heavy oxygen cylinders in buildings with no elevators.

On one occasion as he was dragging a large, heavy cylinder of oxygen up a flight of stairs, the cylinder got away from him and slid back down the stairs much more quickly than Brent could follow. He watched in dismay as it reached the bottom of the stairs and punched a hole in the wall. Thankfully, no one was injured by this errant oxygen missile, and after arranging to repair the wall, delivery resumed.

Brent progressed from being a driver to managing the drivers, then to equipment purchasing and running the warehouse. He eventually became a shareholder, living the mission statement and remaining in the company for many years after I retired.

We had several people who started out as drivers and ended up as shareholders, managers, and even respiratory therapists. We truly believed that our employees were entrusted to us by God and that we were meant to serve them and help them develop their potential. Some of our employees even ended up with doctorates as they grew in their vocations, and their passion and callings matured.

Rudi Radke joined our team when we moved the business into the office warehouse. ARS had grown too big to be run out of our homes, so this was a reasonable next step. Rudi took on the task of office management where his training in business accounting was put to good use.

Rudi recalls meeting several members of the ARS team at a Christmas party in Ralph Sperry's home before beginning to work for us in January of 1983. He was looking for a change from his job with an insurance company, and while attending a Bible study with Terry Zimmerman, was encouraged to consider working for ARS. Terry had come to ARS just before that time and wore several different hats during his time in the business.

The chaos of a new office location didn't scare Rudi away, even when he had to share my desk for his first few days while the offices were being set up and organized.

Elli Zapf gave him an overview of the payroll system while Caroline acquainted him with the billing and receivables. Rudi was a great manager and humbly worked at whatever was needed in the office. He figured out what needed to be done and did a lot of creative problem-solving while overseeing and training our office staff. He became a good friend to me and to many others in the ARS family.

Yaremchuk & Annicchiarico was an accounting firm recommended by a business associate to do our year-end financials. I took all of our material to them, and when the work was completed, Peter Yaremchuk commented that the reason their bill was so high was that they had to spend a lot of time on our books. He wondered whether our accountant was inexperienced or simply overwhelmed by the amount of work he had to do with the business. Experience wasn't the problem, but these comments led us to have Wade Brehm come on staff to help lighten the load. Little did we know that he would become the leader of ARS and take the business to a level I never dreamed of.

In conversations with Wade, I was reminded that he initially joined our staff as a consultant to help us establish accounting systems and better manage personnel. We're grateful that he never left.

As ARS grew, we discovered opportunities to expand into other provinces. We became Alberta Respiratory Services and Associates and then Associated Respiratory Services as we sought to meet the needs of patients in Saskatchewan and British Columbia.

Mac Scott, our head of southern Alberta, and I met with Rick and Bev Snyder in 1983 to ask if they would be willing to relocate to Saskatchewan. At that time, Rick had a secure job as department head of inhalation therapy in a hospital. Rick recalls that after hearing my impassioned vision for accessible oxygen home care, he wanted a few days to think about it. Bev looked squarely at me and said, "You know if Rick doesn't accept the position, I sure will!"

They accepted the challenge of serving the people of Saskatchewan and built a great team there. When I visited Saskatchewan, I saw firsthand the impact they had as they grew to handle 75 to 90 percent of that province's respiratory home care patients. This was not the result of marketing, but because they so wonderfully served their customers. Word travelled, and they had the opportunity to serve hundreds of people.

On one visit, I was able to attend a customer appreciation breakfast they hosted where hundreds of people came to express their gratitude and admiration. On another occasion, I had the privilege of making a home visit with Rick and providing a suction machine to one of Canada's first heart-lung transplant patients.

Some years later, at the Edmonton Airport, I struck up a conversation with an elderly lady. This woman was from Preeceville, SK, and as we spoke, she shared that she was a recent widow who had nursed her late husband through the last stages of a terminal illness. When I shared that I was associated with oxygen home care, this woman reacted with excitement. She shared that the ARS team from Saskatoon had come all the way to Preeceville to arrange oxygen home care for her husband, and she couldn't say enough about the team there. That was the kind of team Rick and Bev built in Saskatchewan.

As we continued meeting needs in the communities we served, we became aware of the need for anaesthesia and medical gas machines in veterinary settings. As early anaesthesia machines became obsolete for human patients, they were in high demand for veterinary use. We acquired some of these machines and refurbished them. A good friend, Stirling Welwood, was looking for work after the downturn in the sheet metal business. He had been involved in building the university hospital and was one of those people who could fix almost anything. He took on the job of serving veterinary clinics all over Western Canada.

Stirling Welwood, AVS technician, checks anesthesia equipment

He would drive his little Toyota from town to town, staying in cheap motels, visiting these clinics and servicing their machinery. It's little wonder the veterinarians and their staff fell in love with this humble fix-it genius who served faithfully and selflessly. Alberta Veterinary Services (AVS) didn't make a lot of money, but it certainly met a need which was all the justification needed to add AVS to our growing business.

As ARS grew, we had hundreds, perhaps thousands, of pieces of equipment in the homes of our patients. When things would break down, or when equipment was returned, it had to be serviced before setting it up for new patients. We had several talented service people who became experts in oxygen concentrators and related equipment. We soon expanded into servicing and selling ventilators and equipment to institutions. The equipment was technologically state of the art, and a respiratory therapist wouldn't know how to service it. However, God provided people with a special knack for repair at just the right time to fill these positions.

Ed Krueger had been in the cement contracting business and was a great friend we knew from church. He stepped in to learn how to service oxygen concentrators and then was able to teach others this very necessary skill. As a major user of this equipment, we had good insight into how to develop better equipment as well as how to more effectively serve our patients.

Ed Krueger works on an oxygen concentrator

We had a front row seat in the life lesson of how God builds things step-by-step as we step out in obedience to do the next thing that lies before us, and as we see a need and seek to respond to it. This was very much how ARS grew; people who were working in the business saw opportunities, and they stepped out to meet needs and do things according to their gifts and talents. I was not the primary visionary in all of this. I simply did what I could to meet the needs I saw, and God brought an amazing team of people around who did the same.

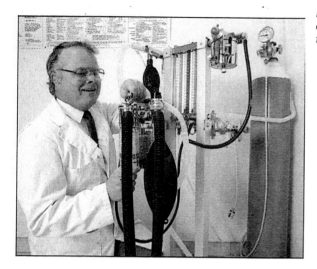

Ken Edwards examines a flow valve

Gord Emerson and Ken Tin examine a liquid oxygen vacuum flask

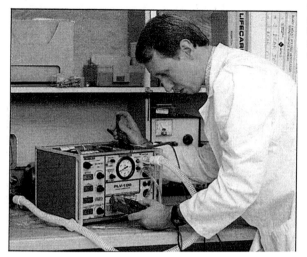

Ken Zeitner performs a calibration test on a ventilator

We all sought to serve our patients and to do our best. It sounds naïve to say that we didn't see ourselves as a business that was out there to make money, but we honestly envisioned ARS as a vehicle to serve and meet the needs of our patients.

As we expanded, this vision carried on. The model I followed was Jesus and seeking to serve and love people as He taught and modelled. This was never really taught to the staff of ARS even though many of the people who came to work with us shared a similar faith and church background in the early days. However, even the staff who did not profess any religious affiliation prioritized patient care and service; there was definitely a shared culture of integrity and seeking to do the right thing. We never made faith or church attendance a requirement for our staff, but God brought likeminded people from many different backgrounds together to build an amazing team.

Mission statements were very popular around that time, and we were encouraged to distill the values of ARS into a summary of business. A team of employees led by Terry Zimmerman, Bev Snyder, Rudi Radke, Wade Brehm, and perhaps some others worked on that project. There were more non-negotiable facets of our mission than would fit into a one-line statement, but we eventually developed something to encapsulate the values we shared:

It is the resolve of ARS to operate its business under the direction of God, recognizing that He is our ultimate authority.

This strong commitment, our attitude towards others, and our stewardship has made us successful as healthcare providers.

We believe that to continue to be successful we are required:

1. To truly care for the patients and customers we serve, not so much out of obligation, but out of a genuine desire to meet their needs.
2. To do that which is right by those we serve in all circumstances.
3. To create an environment where staff have a sincere commitment to one another and have opportunity for personal fulfillment, recognizing that each one is valuable.
4. To recognize that the importance of family and spiritual life is equal to or greater than career and monetary success.
5. To be good stewards of our resources, including our skills, our time, and our material goods, preserving and developing them, and committing them into areas of useful need.

There were definitely challenges as we navigated the government programs that paid for our patients' equipment through Aids to Daily Living. We would find seniors using a nasal cannula that had become as hard as a piece of wood or metal and was irritating the nose. When we asked why the patient wouldn't get a new cannula, we were told that each cannula cost the government $1.65, and our patients were anxious not to cause extra expense to the program. We assured them that replacing these parts every two to four weeks as recommended was certainly not taking advantage of the program.

We also faced the real challenge of physicians ordering things that the program was unwilling to pay for, and several times, we had to go to bat for the patients with the government or improvise a solution that would meet the patient's need while still falling under the program regulations for funding. Sometimes, the rules for funding were changed by the patients themselves when they complained to their political representatives who then made adjustments in government programs. We discovered that who you know is as important as what you know and that government can be swayed if enough people speak out.

We did our best to navigate the realities of our healthcare system, finding solutions for our patients. These people continually inspired us with their fortitude and endurance as they faced circumstances that were often much more difficult than my own had been. I was enriched by seeing God in these homes while we served.

25. The Patients

Over time, God used patients that we were serving to teach me about His character. The first gentleman was one of our early oxygen patients when we had old trucks and we as respiratory therapists were not only initiating the treatment, but also delivering the oxygen.

This man had been a pipefitter in the oil patch, and he was dealing with a terminal illness. His wife was a beautiful evangelical Christian, but our patient didn't present as a typical Christian with his rough manner and colourful language.

During this time, I would often sing scripture songs as I got to know people through being in their homes. I sought to build relationship and would pray for the patients and talk about Jesus as our friendship developed.

One day, I was in a hurry and didn't take the time to sing and pray with this gentleman. I went out to my truck to drive away, but the truck wouldn't start. This was in the days before cell phones, so I went back in the house and asked if I could use their phone. My friend, the patient, said, "Well, you didn't pray for me, and you didn't sing."

"Oh! Let's fix that!" I replied.

I prayed for him and sang, and wouldn't you know that when I went out to my truck again, it started right up.

God was at work in this man even as we treated his physical symptoms. As his disease progressed, he was sent to hospital, and I felt a nudge to go see him. He was nearing the end of his life and was in a semi-comatose state. As I stood by his bedside holding his hand and praying, he opened his eyes and squeezed my hand.

"It's OK," I heard. Whether he said that or whether the spirit of God whispered it to my heart, I don't recall, but I knew he was at peace with God.

Soon thereafter, I had the joy of sharing in the celebration of his life with his family, knowing that he was at rest in the presence of God.

Another patient who deeply affected my life was a lady who had been started on IPPB therapy by my colleague Ralph. There had been no payments on the apparatus she was using, so I called in to see her. When I arrived to speak with her, I noticed that she was smoking.

I told her that smoking was really undermining what the treatment was designed to do for her. She told me that she had just bought the memorial gravestone for her daughter.

God moved my heart for this family, and while we discontinued therapy at her request and with her physician's approval, we were able to pray together and ask God to enter her circumstances. Later, a group of us came to pray for her healing, and while we didn't see a physical healing, we knew that God was working in her life. Later when she was on oxygen, she and her husband were facing some challenges. When I visited, I asked whether she would like Jesus to change that relationship. She said yes, we prayed, and Jesus came into her situation.

After her passing when I came to pick up the equipment, her family embraced me saying, "You are welcome in our home anytime." We fulfilled the physician's prescription and offered our services, but God came into their situation offering much more than any of us anticipated. They were a Jewish family, and I saw the joy and peace of God helping them through an exceedingly challenging time. What a privilege to walk with people and participate with the Spirit of God.

God uses wonderful people to teach you about yourself as well as your vocation. Annie was one of these people. A young Indigenous teenager with a new baby, and very serious lung disease, Annie became one of our patients. Her diagnosis was bronchiectasis; recurrent pulmonary infections had already destroyed sufficient lung tissue that she was unable to maintain livable oxygen levels without supplemental oxygen. We became her oxygen supplier.

Annie lived in rental apartments, and it was not uncommon to discover that our oxygen truck not only delivered oxygen to her but also served as a moving truck when she needed to change her living arrangements.

Annie was beautiful. When she smiled, the whole room lit up. She had a wonderful, joyful disposition despite the challenges of dealing with serious health issues. She loved her little daughter, who was an active toddler. When we would deliver oxygen cylinders to the home, we had to make sure the tanks were laid down since the danger of these large, heavy cylinders falling on the small child before we could secure them was a real concern.

In winter, I recall laying a frosty oxygen tank on the floor and going out to get a second one. When I returned, the little toddler would be sitting on the cylinder, often bare-bummed; the life-saving oxygen was such a fixture in the home that it was like a piece of furniture!

Annie looked to God for a solution to her clinical reality, and a couple of us accompanied her to a faith healing meeting. Annie was not lacking faith, but God did not heal her lung condition at that meeting. When we returned to her home, she tore the oxygen cannula from her face in despair and ran out into the night. Dennis, the other staff member who had come to the meeting with us, ran after her. When he returned to the apartment some time later carrying Annie's small, limp figure, she was dusky with oxygen deprivation. She was almost comatose, and I feared we had lost her. We administered oxygen, and she came around. While God did not heal her, she did not succumb to hypoxia that night.

Not long after this experience, I received a call from her physician's office. This was the same doctor who had objected to my interference during my brother-in-law's hospitalization a few years earlier. Over the phone came a hostile voice: "I understand that you are introducing God into Annie's treatment?!?"

I responded, "Do you get distress calls at 4:30 in the morning when she's out of oxygen? Are you aware that she might be pregnant because she's sleeping with people who may not have her best interests at heart?"

These realities were what I experienced when I went to her apartment at 4:00 a.m. one morning to find a young man smoking in her bed with the oxygen running into the bedding.

Would you believe this young fellow was someone I had the privilege of meeting in the Yukon in 1958? Needless to say, he got quite a lecture on his activities and the hazards of mixing oxygen and smoking.

Annie's condition continued to deteriorate until she required hospitalization. When she was on a ventilator at the university hospital, I became aware that the health system was working to return her to British Columbia, the province of her birth. We helped her move, and she became a client of another oxygen home care company in Vancouver.

The next time I received a phone call from Annie, she asked me to come visit her in hospital. She shared with me some of the background regarding her move back to BC.

Apparently, a family in Vancouver with a ministry of adopting children who needed care had sought to adopt her as a child. The authorities refused and sent her back to the Indigenous community where her health declined. Even though they had not been allowed to adopt Annie, this family continued to advocate for her. They pressured the government on her behalf until the province of British Columbia admitted their culpability in her declining health and assumed all costs for her care.

In later years, Annie married one of our oxygen delivery drivers. She asked if we could provide some suction catheters for her which we happily did, and she thanked me for our friendship.

Annie affected my life deeply as I saw the challenges of severe disease, the resilience of an amazing character, and some of the pitfalls and failures of our healthcare system. That was my last contact with Annie, but I hope to have opportunity to catch up with her when I leave this world as she has, to join our Savior.

26. Little Red Wagon

My first vehicle with ARS was a red four-cylinder diesel Land Cruiser. At this time, we also purchased a white Toyota Cressida for Gerry to use as our family car. We never really separated our business life from our personal life and that may become evident and may be fodder for critics with other opinions.

I remember my first drive in the red Land Cruiser. I noticed in the test drive that there were small pocks or pits in the windshield that may have been the result of environmental pollution. As a real negotiator, I insisted that Toyota change the windshield which they were happy to do. On my first trip with ARS out of town heading towards Redwater, I encountered a gravel truck without a tarp on it. It may have also been loose gravel in his tires. In any case, as we passed each other, a large stone landed right in the middle of my windshield, shattering it into a million pieces. None of the pieces penetrated the glass surface, but the windshield needed to be replaced. This was my first lesson that the manufacturer's little defect was nothing compared to the risks out on the road. I fell in love with this vehicle but was to discover I still had a lot to learn about the object of my affection.

Number one: a four-cylinder diesel does not have the same power as an eight-cylinder gas vehicle. I tried to pass a gravel truck, thinking I had plenty of room to do so. This would have been the case with an eight-cylinder, but as I drove up beside the truck, the oncoming traffic came more quickly than I was able to pull ahead, and I ended up straddling the centre line. The driver of the gravel truck and the driver of the oncoming vehicle each moved over a bit, and we avoided a head-on collision. That experience may have shortened my life a bit, and I may have wet my pants, but I lived to learn the next lesson.

My "little red wagon" was my first four-wheel drive, and during a wild winter storm in Edmonton one year, I had the chance to test it out. I was driving to work on 118th Avenue during one of the worst storms we had experienced. My little red wagon ended up in the ditch along with some other vehicles including an Edmonton Transit bus. When the tow truck arrived to render assistance, I was backing up and going forward but not getting out of the ditch. This was disappointing since

I had expected that a four-wheel drive could go anywhere! The tow truck driver came to my window and said, "Your front wheels are not turning."

I had forgotten that I needed to lock them in by maneuvering something at the wheel in order for the vehicle to function in four-wheel drive. I locked the wheels and drove right out of the ditch, leaving the bus and tow trucks to deal with the carnage of the storm. I got to work just fine.

The next day when I went to work, I discovered my little red wagon on the front page of the Edmonton Journal. My staff had cut out the picture and written "Our Fearless Leader Beat the Storm."

Another occasion I will never forget was when I was looking after patients in the Westlock-Barrhead area. I discovered that the oxygen depot needed to be moved to a new location. I loaded sixteen H cylinders in the back of that little red wagon, put seventy pounds of air pressure in the tires, and drove a few miles before discovering that the front wheels were hardly on the ground due to the weight of the cylinders in the back. We made it, and I was once again impressed by that little vehicle.

One of my most memorable adventures with the little red wagon occurred when I was starting a patient on oxygen in a little community west of Drayton Valley. I got the referral and started on my journey with all of the required equipment. As I travelled on Highway 39 between Leduc and Drayton Valley, I encountered a natural phenomenon that was new to me.

It had been raining steadily in that area for a week, and I was confronted by water running over the highway for half a mile. The water was about six inches deep, and I could see that it had washed out a part of a farmyard on one side of the road. I was able to drive that half-mile of road by straddling the centre line, but when I reached Drayton Valley, the RCMP were stopping traffic from crossing over the river. I explained my situation, and the police said I could try crossing over the bridge.

The bridge surface was safe, but water was flowing over it. Never one to back down from a challenge, I naïvely decided to try it. Halfway across the bridge, the water came up on the side of my Land Cruiser, and the vehicle stalled. I glanced to the left and saw a car a few hundred yards down in the creek bed that had obviously been washed over by the surge of water. I uttered a quick prayer and tried to start my vehicle. The diesel engine started, and I proceeded to cross the bridge safely, giving thanks that God had answered my prayer despite my foolishness in attempting such a crazy thing. I reached the little community, found my patient, and started him on oxygen before heading back to Edmonton.

While passing the golf course on my way home, I noticed that it was one big water hazard. In fact, I encountered water over the road in at least five different places and had to guess at where the road was as I journeyed home. That great little vehicle made it, despite the questionable skills of its driver, and I was grateful to have been able to look after that patient despite the road conditions.

Another story involving my little red wagon occurred when I was looking after patients in British Columbia. I left Edmonton at four in the afternoon, needing to get to Kamloops for activities the following day. Between Jasper and Kamloops, there was a severe snowstorm which made visibility very poor.

I was following the snow ploughs and making good progress until I reached a community about 100 km from Kamloops. Three deer suddenly appeared in my view, crossing the road. I was travelling at a maximum safe speed, and as I hit my brakes, two of the deer made it safely across, but the third collided directly with its right shoulder into my left headlight. The animal disappeared into the ditch, and I continued into the community to find the RCMP and obtain an accident sticker.

The RCMP officer asked whether I had killed the deer, and I honestly didn't know, but judging from the damage to my vehicle, I thought it probable. The officer informed me that in that area there had been sixty deer killed that winter. One year, we experienced eight of our ARS vehicles being damaged in collisions with deer. I'm not sure whether the deer were attempting to mate with our vehicles or put in a request for oxygen, but we had a lot of experience trying to get to our destinations in Western Canada under trying circumstances.

The final story I want to tell about my little red wagon occurred when I was working in Victoria, BC, and wanted to get home to Edmonton in time for a Christmas party. I had taken the ferry across to the mainland and was part way through a long day of driving when I reached the summit of the Coquihalla. As I headed down into the communities that were at a lower elevation, the weather vacillated between freezing snow and freezing rain.

I had already worked a twelve-hour day and should have called it a day, but I really wanted to get home. As I was leaving Merritt and climbing up to Kamloops, my little red wagon was in cruise control, and I hit some black ice. I didn't handle it too well. I hit the brakes, and the vehicle skidded sideways into the median that separated the highway with traffic going in the opposite direction. The wagon went down into the median between the lanes of traffic, sliding sideways and then rolling over the resulting buildup of snow. The vehicle finished its wild ride upside-down, with me hanging from my seatbelt, surveying the broken window, and grateful that the ride was over. I was acutely aware that God had saved me from an accident that could have been much worse.

I managed to turn off the engine which was still running and release my seatbelt which dropped me unceremoniously out of the seat and onto the broken glass that covered the inside of the vehicle. By the time I extricated myself from the vehicle and confirmed that I had no injuries, people had called 9-1-1, and the police and ambulance crew were there to help me. The tow truck took me to Kamloops where my son Evan was studying, and from his place, I was able to rent a car to drive to Edmonton.

My little red wagon was loaded up and brought back to Edmonton where the insurance company wrote it off since the cost of repairing it would have exceeded its value. The vehicle had about 250,000 km on it, but I couldn't bear to part with it. I don't remember how much the insurance company paid us for the vehicle, but I bought it back from them and had Carl Kochen straighten the frame and repair it. I drove it for another hundred kilometers and then sold it to a sports person who may still be driving it.

The last time I saw my little red wagon was when I stopped at Dead Man's Flats on the way to Banff. I stopped at the motel service station there and spied the wagon with the hood up which allowed me to look at the engine. I noticed the gaskets were leaking oil and struck up a conversation with the owner to ascertain that it really was my little red wagon. "You need to fix those gaskets, and this vehicle will drive another million kilometers if you just look after it," was my advice. I have no idea where that little wagon is today, but if I ever see it again, I will probably buy it back!

27. Canadian Liquid Air and Oxygen Agreements

As I talk about the changes that occurred in our life with entering the home care business, it might sound like all we did was work. The truth is that we did work a lot, but there also came a corresponding change in our net worth. The business was doing well, and we saw the proof of that growth in the financial statements.

I have always believed that my life belongs to God, and therefore that our business belonged to God. God does not need a business, but he often uses these life experiences to grow us into the people He desires us to be. One of the challenges that we faced was that most of the work that we did was compensated through the government oxygen programs. Our relationship with the oxygen supplier Canadian Liquid Air (CLA) was not optimal.

As mentioned earlier, our need for an oxygen supplier for our home care patients led us to make an agreement with CLA. The Royal Alex Hospital had a contract with CLA which meant this was the company with which I was most familiar. We chose them as our oxygen supplier, having little understanding of the importance of this supply agreement.

While they were a good manufacturer, they still did not have the kind of service that our growing business needed. I spent some time thinking of changing our oxygen supplier, but it was doubtful that another company would provide better service. While pondering this, we came to the realization that the oxygen supply agreement with CLA was really an acquisition agreement. If something happened to Don and Gerry Smailes, Canadian Liquid Air had the first option to purchase the business. This caused us to look at whether we should, in fact, sell some of the business to CLA. We eventually did sell 35 percent of the business to them, and I don't remember the amount of the sale, but it was the first time I've seen cheques that had millions of dollars on them. That drastically changed things.

One of the biggest changes was that our lawyers informed us that in selling these shares, the law allowed us to gift some shares to our children to minimize our tax burden. Gerry and I each contributed $200,000 and when divided among our three children, it provided each of them about $133,000 which was enough to help with purchasing their first homes. This was a great blessing to us and to our kids, and reflected God's abundant provision for our family.

At that time, we were also able to invite some key employees into ownership of the business by allowing them to purchase shares at a discounted rate. Payment for the shares would come out of the earnings of the shares themselves as they were transferred to the original owners.

We selected the original seven shareholders based on their demonstrated excellence of ability in their jobs and their willingness to take on responsibility. They were our management people who were already key players in the organization. They had a significant track record of employment and were willing to take on the opportunity to have a voice in how the company developed. The original seven were Don Smailes, Wade Brehm, Ralph Sperry, Rick Snyder, Mac Scott, Terry Zimmerman, and Brent Smailes.

The concept of freezing the assets and opening ownership to more people was based on my personal spiritual journey. I have often said that the business belongs to God, and as my personal spiritual journey progressed, I realized that in a sense God owns everything and calls us as stewards through the various interests, opportunities and challenges that come into our lives. He doesn't need a business, but He uses these opportunities to form character and to produce the results that He has in mind. That was definitely my understanding of what the kingdom of God is like and how it was to be lived out in my personal life. God was very faithful in providing the people that we needed to accomplish the purpose He had called us to, and now was the occasion to transfer further opportunity and responsibility to those people.

As an evangelical Christian, I had certain concepts of what being a Christian entailed in terms of lifestyle and doctrine, and God was in the process of making some adjustments to my understanding. I struggled with the selection of two of the candidates who had come up for this employee ownership opportunity: one was a manager who was not performing his responsibilities well, and he graciously declined the offer to become a shareholder.

The second person had a different lifestyle than I did, which I judged as not as godly as my own. I met with this man and his wife, and as we shared on a heart level, I was convicted of my judgmental spirit and became convinced that he should be one of the original seven shareholders. History confirmed that this was not merely a wise decision but one that blessed me and the company greatly. This person not only made substantial contributions as a manager, respiratory therapist, and leader, but two of his sons also worked in the business in later years. I had the privilege of learning from this family.

Because we looked at our business as belonging to God, we were also able to gift to charitable organizations from the profits that were being generated by the business.

With the sale of part of the business to CLA, I did not feel comfortable making the decision of donating to charity for the entire business. It was one thing for Gerry and me to give from our personal earnings, but I recognized that not everyone in the business would choose to dispense funds this way. When I talked to our lawyer, Rick Ewasiuk, he informed me that it would be possible to form a charitable foundation. We could then transfer some of our shares to the charity and could be reimbursed by the company for the cost of the shares, passing on to the charity, tax free, the growth of the value of the shares. When the company was able to afford to redeem these shares, Don and Gerry Smailes would receive a receipt for $8.33 (the cost of the shares) and the charity would receive $50,000 (the actual value of the shares). God was so gracious in surrounding us with people who had wisdom and knowledge in areas that helped us to be good stewards of His financial blessings.

The influx of capital also allowed us to remove the bank as the lender to our business. We were able to finance the growth of the business, and the business paid us a fee less than what the bank was charging us.

As God increased our resources, we also became aware of the Cambodian genocide and the resulting refugee challenges. We sponsored a family from Cambodia, and when they arrived in Canada along with some other people, they were employed at ARS. It became evident that the differences in culture were a major challenge for these newcomers to Canada in finding employment.

We took the opportunity to form a company called Helping Hands. We hired two people to oversee this operation and started two businesses out of it to provide employment: a janitorial service and a landscape and yard maintenance service. Our hired staff really had a heart for these people and devoted tremendous energy trying to find work for the companies, as well as helping the refugees adjust to life in Canada. There was no direct supervision from ARS, but we did handle the books.

After a period of time, we realized that this endeavour was costing a lot of money. The bills amounted to a loss of $250,000. We recognized that we could not afford to continue subsidizing this and decided to split Helping Hands into the two businesses, allowing the Cambodians to run them independently. The Christian workers rose to the challenge of finding new employment and both companies managed quite well without our help. This experience was a great lesson in learning how expensive and challenging it is to help people from another culture adjust to life in a new country. Fortunately, the losses were tax deductible and provided some relief from the heavy tax burden on a profitable business.

28. Wolves in Sheep's Clothing

I don't think any of us knew exactly what God was building as our team came together and expanded in ARS. Various leadership members invited people to join the business according to the needs in their areas of responsibility. I did this as well, but unfortunately some of the people I invited to join the team were discovered to be "wolves in sheep's clothing." People can pretend to be something they are not, sometimes not even realizing the truth of their own character. However, life and our interactions with others eventually reveal the hidden things in each heart.

One of the invitees to the ARS team was cause for deep regret and many lessons learned. We met at church during the time we were involved in Helping Hands.

Mr. Jones offered to do a business analysis of that ministry. He did a good job of that, and we consequently made decisions to turn the ministry over to the refugees themselves for management.

Over the course of providing this analysis, Mr. Jones suggested that there were probably inefficiencies in our ARS business that he could help remedy. I invited him onto the team where he quickly insinuated himself into management positions. In retrospect, he was very deliberate and adept at inserting himself in beneficial relationships, and I confess that I trusted him because he professed to be a Christian.

In retrospect, my spiritual and religious orientation coloured my perceptions and blurred my judgment. In fact, other people in the company who didn't have those same religious blinders saw things that I couldn't or didn't see, but they were hesitant to say anything to me because of the common bond of faith they believed Mr. Jones and I shared. This made Mr. Jones practically untouchable, and he proceeded into management for our BC operation, quickly moving towards becoming a shareholder in the company.

Luke 8:17 says, "For there is nothing hidden that will not be disclosed, and nothing concealed that will not be known or brought out into the open."

Information began to filter in on the activities of this man, and an investigation began. During a trip to Saskatoon for shareholder meetings, God showed me at nighttime what was happening with Mr. Jones. We then had a lawyer investigate the matter, talking to our staff members who had dealings with Mr. Jones. The investigation uncovered blackmail and many despicable things that were being done to our employees without our knowledge.

The confrontation with Mr. Jones was not pretty. He had been seeing a cardiologist for health reasons, and this seemed an apt metaphor as we tried to deal with heart issues of another sort.

As the investigation progressed, we found that he had done this to other businesses in Alberta before coming to Edmonton. What bothered me the most was that he professed to be a follower of Jesus. I believed he was, but when the fruit of his life came to light, it was difficult to reconcile his profession of faith with his actions. As a result, many people were injured by his evil activities and perhaps even soured by the witness of this so-called Christian. It's very hard to undo these kinds of actions and consequences, but I'm thankful that God brought his actions to light before he could totally destroy the company.

Al Sperry and our lawyers helped to rescue the business in British Columbia. The efforts of Wendy Marlow, Gwen Chapman, Deb Spildee, and team under Rick Snyder, Wade Brehm, and Al Sperry put the business back on track with living the mission statement. The team there was eventually rebuilt, but I still shudder to think that it was almost destroyed by someone I invited into the business. Despite good intentions, leaders make mistakes too.

God used this experience in ARS to reveal my religious prejudices in much the same way that He challenged me when I worked at the Royal Alex with the nuns who came to be orientated to the respiratory equipment they used in their hospitals. God used them to show me that their love for Jesus was just like mine. I soon found myself becoming an advocate for Catholics among Protestants who, because of fear and unfounded gossip stories, were spreading untruths. God used my exposure to patients in the home care area to show me how big He was. I went into homes where the language was offensive to me, but I found God present in ways that I never imagined.

As the company continued to grow, we looked at expanding into Eastern Canada. VitalAire, the medical branch of the French company

Air Liquide which owned Canadian Liquid Air, was already active in this part of the country. We had some meetings with VitalAire to discuss a merger. ARS had the structure and experience in providing respiratory home care, while VitalAire had a much wider sphere of influence and connections across the country, and worldwide. This was a big step for our company, and in my excitement over the possibilities I almost got us in trouble with the competition bureau. There was a concern that merging these two respiratory businesses would give VitalAire a monopoly on respiratory home care. In my mind, it didn't make sense to compete when we could accomplish so much more together.

We ended up in a partnership after several meetings and the agreement that Don Smailes should keep his mouth shut when it came to talking about the finer points of the business, since I sometimes lacked wisdom in what I said and to whom I spoke.

During the meetings with VitalAire, the CEO asked me how I thought things were going.

"We're a long way from Beatty!" was my reply.

It was astounding to look back at how far this scrawny farm kid had come. Sometime after that, our accountants and lawyer informed me that Gerry's and my equity in the business would be sufficient for early retirement if I was ready to step off into a new adventure. I recognized that ARS/VitalAire required a different kind of leadership for this new chapter than what I was able to provide.

We had a staff meeting scheduled in Banff and, as Wade Brehm and I travelled to the mountains, we had a wonderful conversation. I shared that I saw him as the next executive leader. There was no desire or ambition on his part for a change in leadership, but I had a sense that God was releasing me from the business.

That night in the hotel, I went to bed, sleeping soundly until about two in the morning. I woke with the sense that God wanted to speak to me. As I went out to walk the streets of Banff, a scripture verse from John 12:24 was impressed upon me: "Unless a grain of wheat falls into the earth and dies, it remains alone; but if it dies, it bears much fruit." (ESV)

With tears running down my face, I realized this was God's confirmation that our leadership change was to occur. I shared that with our staff the next day, and it began the transition of my retirement.

I continued to be involved on the board for some time, and still enjoy relationship with some of the wonderful people who became like family as we worked together. In hindsight, the hand of God was so obvious in choosing amazing people at the right time to allow ARS/VitalAire to develop into what it became. We thought we were selecting staff members on the basis of who was available when different needs arose. Certainly, I was no mastermind CEO who knew how to build such a team. But God didn't call me to know everything about His business. My job was to do what He gave me the ability to do while He gathered a team around me and let us participate in building something beyond our wildest dreams.

29. Adventures on the Ski Hill

Lest you get the impression that all we did was work and engage in charitable endeavours, let me assure you that we had some fun holiday and family time in the midst of everything else. One family holiday, we went with my sister Pat and her husband Don and their family to the Shuswap area in British Columbia. We stayed in a timeshare there and had a wonderful vacation enjoying the water and good company. On our way home from that experience, we drove through the East Kootenays and stopped in at Panorama Resort. By the time we had finished looking around, we were the proud owners of two weeks in a timeshare at Panorama.

We became interested in the sport of skiing around this time since one of our timeshare weeks was in the winter. Gerry and I were in our early forties when we bought the timeshare, and we discovered that you cannot be near the ski hill without taking up skiing. We enrolled in the ski school and had a lot of fun learning in a group with other people of the same (lack of) ability as ourselves. We all became friends and learned together.

It's an interesting experience to be on a ski hill where gravity is pulling you downhill and you have these boards on your feet that seem to have a mind of their own at times. I remember the embarrassment of gliding up to a lady that I didn't know and having my skis go between hers until we found ourselves face-to-face.

The young ski instructor said, "Now is a good time to ask for her phone number!"

My wife didn't agree, so I extricated myself and eventually learned how to harness these contrary boards. By the end of the week, we participated in a ski race which was a lot of fun. We also ended up with a diploma and improved skiing abilities.

Panorama was the place we were introduced to hot tubs. There's nothing better to get the aches out of a hurting body than hot water and good company. Skiing caused me to enjoy winter as I loved the view of the mountains, the thrill of speed skiing down the hills, and the exhilaration of being outdoors breathing crisp, cool air.

A couple of our respiratory colleagues, Neil Patterson and Lorne White, were accomplished skiers and had even been part of the ski patrol at Jasper, Alberta. I remember someone asking them whether I was a good skier, and their reply was, "I wouldn't say good, I would say fast!"

Somehow, I thought the object was to get to the bottom of the hill as quickly as possible and then up the mountain again to see if I could do better the next time.

Before attempting downhill skiing, our family had tried cross-country skiing. The only thing that I enjoyed about that was when we came to a hill where I could activate gravity and get up some speed. Downhill skiing was a natural progression to satisfy my need for speed.

Evan had made the transition from playing hockey to skiing, and wanting to keep up with my kids was a great stimulus to get me involved in the sport. I'm surely not the only one willing to risk life and limb to keep up with young people. Once I entered pre-retirement and had the freedom and time to spend on these kinds of activities, I became the chaperone for Evan and his friends Randy, Sheldon, and Brad.

The first time I tried downhill skiing was at Red Mountain in Trail, BC. I remember going on the chair lift for the first time and being grateful to manage getting on the chair without crashing. As we went up the mountain, I was in awe that we were hundreds of feet above the ground. I wondered how we would ever get down if the lift stopped. We reached the top and then I had to deal with the mountain taking me places I wasn't sure I wanted to go. The only thing that saved me was remembering what I had done when I couldn't stop while skating. It was a great motivation to improve my skills.

When we went to Red Mountain the next time, we were renting a suite from a charming, single English woman who was a guide on the ski hill. Upon arriving at our lodging that evening, we discovered that she had a party going on with her friends. The main event was skinny dipping in the hot tub, and the window of our suite afforded a clear view of naked young men and women heading to the hot tub.

As the chaperone and a deacon of the church, I had to think fast while these young men in my charge gaped at the display of flesh right outside the window. We drew the blinds and went to sleep. I'm not sure whether the boys shared anything with their parents about this part of the trip, but I do know that it wasn't brought up in the deacons meeting.

Evan and buddies on a ski trip

Our host turned out to be an exceptional skier, and she took the boys, who were good skiers, onto the backside of the mountain where they experienced skiing like they never had before. When it came time to get in the hot tub after skiing, we opted to wear swimming trunks!

I have the dubious honour of being the champion of ski destruction in our family. This was not a planned accomplishment, but over the years, I wore out or destroyed at least five sets of skis in various accidents. When Evan was studying respiratory therapy in Kamloops, his favourite ski area was Todd Mountain which is now known as Sun Peaks.

I remember Evan and his buddies taking me up to the top of that mountain and deciding that they would ski out of bounds because the powder was so deep and inviting. I had never skied in powder and did not know how to manage this experience. In retrospect, I should have stayed on the groomed runs, but not being one to miss out on a challenge, I ventured into the deep snow.

I could not control my skis and quickly lost one ski. By the time I was able to stop, I was some one hundred feet down the mountain and had to climb back up to retrieve the lost ski. Crawling up a forty-five-degree slope in snow that was over my head and very soft brought me as close to a cardiac arrest as I ever want to come. Some people don't learn very quickly to operate within their limits, and I am a perfect example of that sort of person.

Todd Mountain has some of the longest runs of any ski hill I had ever skied, and it was just wonderful to cruise on these runs. I recall vividly being out there one spring skiing with Rob Jeske and Evan. They were having great fun skiing around moguls and into areas where I was unable to control my skis, so I decided to leave the boys and find some fun of my own.

I glided across an open space, and the next thing I knew, my skis were stuck in an ice bank and I had ejected about twenty feet past the end of the skis. I picked myself up, thankful to be uninjured, and went to retrieve my skis from the ice. I proceeded down the mountain but seemed to have lost all ability to harness the boards on my feet. I wanted to go one direction, and they were determined to go another.

This persisted for some time until I went to Panorama for some skiing and asked the ski technician, Lusty, to see if he could fix my disobedient skis. He gave me a set of loaner skis, and when I came down the mountain at the end of day, he informed me that my skis were unfixable. They had been bent six inches out of their original form and that was why I couldn't control them. Those were the first set of skis destroyed by me running into things that the skis were not designed to navigate.

It's sometimes not a good idea to be skiing with young people when you are over forty and just beginning to develop your abilities. Skiing along the edge of a ski run is dangerous because off to the side are these little runs that seem to hatch and eject small children right into your path. When these little kamikaze skiers burst out of the bushes right in front of you, your risk of injury while trying to avoid them is significant. These diminutive skiers are generally equipped with helmets, but I never skied with a helmet until after I had a few accidents. As I said, some of us require a few more lessons in the school of hard knocks than others.

The most memorable accident happened at Panorama just before Gerry's and my twenty-fifth wedding anniversary. We had been skiing, and some of our party had already left to head back to Edmonton. Randy Hayashi, Evan, and I decided to ski until the ski hill closed for the day. I was skiing with these young, accomplished skiers, and Randy was using a snowboard while Evan was on skis. They were doing jumps on little moguls on the runs, and I decided that I should try that. Not a good decision.

When I came off the mogul, I fell and felt a pulling in my abdomen like I had pulled some muscles. I realized how foolish I had been and just took off down the mountain at a very good speed. I think the run was called Little Dipper, and as I was going down at about a forty-five-degree angle at full speed, I failed to realize that there was a road across the run where the groomers moved equipment. This caused me to go on a level place for about twenty feet until the hill returned to a forty-five-degree angle again. I flew about thirty feet in the air and landed on my right ski which snapped off. Then I hit the surface of the mountain with my shoulder and knew I was in real trouble.

By the time the boys came, I had managed to get back up on my feet and make my way with one ski to the ski lift. The ski patrol loaded me on a toboggan that took me to their headquarters at the base of the main lift. This happened at about 2:30 in the afternoon, and I told the boys, "You carry on skiing until 4 o'clock when the mountain closes and pick me up at the ski patrol office."

By the time they finished skiing, my body was in such pain, I could hardly walk and couldn't even take a deep breath. We were travelling home in Randy's station wagon and decided to stop at the hospital in Invermere to see if they could do something for my pain. All the way down the mountain at every turn and bump, all Evan and Randy heard were my groans and yelps.

When we got to the hospital, they gave me some pain killers but said there really wasn't much they could do for broken ribs. They advised seeing my family doctor when I returned to Edmonton which I did. X-rays confirmed that I had broken my ribs at the place they attach to the spine, which meant it took me half an hour to get out of bed in the morning. I was seeing a chiropractor, one of my former respiratory colleagues, who tried his best to get my bones back in place, but he had limited experience with this type of injury.

My doctor informed me that I had developed bronco-pneumonia and that the best thing would be to rest. Gerry and I had planned a one-month holiday cruise to the Caribbean and Florida to celebrate our anniversary. We got on the plane and that time cruising and relaxing was exactly what my body needed to heal. By the end of our holiday,

I was even able to golf again and had learned that I needed to take better care of myself while skiing.

Later in life, Len Johnson became one of my skiing buddies. I had always wanted to try heli-skiing, and Len and I tried it in the Bugaboos near Panorama. We practised on the runs at Panorama using bigger, wider skis, but it really didn't prepare me for the powder we would encounter up on the mountains where no one had skied before.

The day for our heli-skiing arrived, and we were surprised to find a film crew on the helicopter with us. It was certain they weren't there to film our debatable skiing abilities! On our way up to the glacier, we flew over the areas where a movie had been filmed about the tragedy of a soccer team from the Andes who had lost their lives in a plane crash in the mountains. We arrived at the glacier and it was awesome, with miles of untracked snow to ski down.

At lunchtime, we stopped at a little lake high up in the mountains. As we were there, we began singing "Show Me the Way to Go Home," and I seemed to be the one who best recalled the words and sang loudest. Unbeknownst to me, the film crew captured the singing as we were sitting around the lake.

Later the next day, the film crew ran what they had captured on a Much Music TV program in Ontario. My niece, Kim Smailes, was watching the program and recognized my voice. "That's my Uncle Donnie singing!" she exclaimed. You never know what note-oriety can come out of these innocent ski experiences.

My second heli-skiing adventure was with my son Evan. This time we were not able to go up onto the glaciers due to inclement weather, so we skied in the trees on the mountain where there were no runs.

Again, there was deep powder which, combined with my skiing ability, meant that I spent most of the time digging out of deep snowbanks, searching for my skis, and trying to figure out why I continued to do such foolish things.

Evan had a great day and at the end of our trip professed, "Dad, this is the best day of my life!"

What more could a dad ask for?

30. Panorama

Panorama. Just speaking the word brings back many wonderful memories. As I would walk around the area and look at the mountains during our time-share weeks there, it felt like comparing heaven to the earth of our regular life in the city. It was worlds apart from the prairie beauty of my childhood in Saskatchewan. Our family immediately loved this new place and wanted to spend more time there. As our financial situation continued to improve, we dared to dream of buying property in Panorama.

A realtor told us of a chalet for sale in the residential subdivision. The house was owned by a widow whose husband had died while skiing at Panorama, and she was wanting to relocate. The cabin had everything you could desire in a holiday property, and we decided to remove some funds from our investment in ARS/VitalAire in order to purchase it. I may have even been in British Columbia doing ARS/Vitalaire work when our lawyers completed the transaction. This became our second home.

There were decks and large windows on the main level and even a deck outside the master bedroom on the third floor that provided beautiful vistas to the north. The mountain view was really something special. In addition to the scenery, we were introduced to a variety of wildlife.

Hummingbirds would come and buzz you if you ventured out without a hat. The stellar jay, British Columbia's provincial bird, was a frequent visitor. Moose and deer would come to eat the willow in the yard. You could ski from the ski hill right to the back door on the south side. We soon installed a hot tub back there and began the work that goes with having a second home in the mountains.

We looked at this property as also belonging to God, and the cabin became a shared home with our friends and family who treated it as their home too. One family would book a week or two at the cabin and while they were there, they would strip the deck and repaint it with the preservative that was required.

When we made the six-hour drive from Edmonton to the mountain, we would make a game of guessing how many animals we would see between Banff and Panorama. I think the record was sixty-seven deer in one trip! It was a wonderful place of calm and peace from the challenges and stressors that so often characterized our life in the city!

Christmas was a great celebration time at Panorama, but we did not always go there for the holidays. One of the things that we learned is that having a home 600 km from where you live does not exempt that home from mechanical failures and other problems that homeowners face. It was distressing to have the Radke family go to Panorama one Christmas only to find when they arrived that the furnace had failed and everything was frozen up. As good friends, they embraced the task of getting people out to fix things, and it was obviously a Christmas they will never forget.

Rudi Radke was, in fact, the trustee of our estate, and a very capable office manager for ARS/VitalAire. He is a great decision-maker and person who gets things done, and we joke that having the furnace quit over Christmas couldn't have happened to a better person! I realize again how in so many ways, through our church and through the business, we were just a big family. So many of the people who were a part of our life were not only friends but brothers and sisters in Christ that formed a wonderful extended family.

To the north of Panorama, there's a mountain that boasts an abandoned silver and copper mine at the top. The name of it was Paradise Mine, but it was a play on words with the sign showing a pair of dice used for gambling. The story of this road up to Panorama really involves the silver mine and the copper that was being mined there as well. Apparently, it was a very prosperous mine during the Second World War which caused the road to be built. Story has it that the owner of the mine was rich enough that he would actually slaughter a cow and use the hide to transport concentrated ore from the mountain mine down to the road for further processing.

We made a number of trips up to this mine with our little red Land Cruiser. It was a journey that made you trust in God as much as in the driver of the four-wheel drive to get to the top of the mountain. Often when we had guests, we made this trip way up the mountain to a waterfall where you could stop. We have some pictures of our children bathing under the waterfall.

Don practising his swing off the mountain in Panorama

The trail was one that required a four-wheel drive vehicle. When you got to the top, you could actually drive down the other side of the mountain and enter Invermere from a different direction. I remember hiking from the mine site further up the mountain, and on the way, encountering the largest deer I have ever seen in my life. It was the size of an elk, and its antlers were probably five feet across. When this creature ran out of the bush ahead of me, I realized I would not like to encounter this animal when it was protecting its domain. I would much rather have it run away because I had entered its home.

As you climbed up from the mine and looked to the west, you could see lakes that had glaciers floating in them. I had never seen anything like this in my entire life. Another happening at Panorama was an infestation of pine beetles or some insect that affected the forest. It killed the trees, predominantly affecting spruce trees and perhaps some pine trees. When this happened, I was already retired and had my eye on a second vocation as a tree cutter. I often joke that Saskatchewan used to be a forest, before I learned how to chainsaw, it became a prairie. Of course, that is a joke. Off one of the ski runs close to the timeshare units at Panorama were hundreds and perhaps thousands of dead trees. I said to the staff at Panorama, "I will cut down those trees if you like."

No one stopped me, so I purchased a chainsaw and began cutting down the dead trees. To this day, I am unable to get the tree to come down where I want it to fall. I am not a good "tree feller," despite all the experience I have cutting down trees. I wanted the trees to fall down the mountain, which was facing north, but they insisted on falling south and up the mountain. I would cut them into lengths and then tumble them down the mountain.

By the time we finished our time at Panorama, I had the largest woodpile in that part of BC. I must admit that I was having fun, but it was not necessarily fun for Gerry who had no idea whether a tree had fallen on me or not until I arrived back at the cabin at the end of the day. This was before the era of cell phones, but even if I had possessed a cell phone at that time, those who know me realize that I would still forget to use it to set my family's mind at ease. In any case, I had a lot of fun expanding my woodpile experience from those early days in Saskatchewan and beginning my love affair with chainsaws.

Panorama also became a place to experience white water rafting down the Toby Creek. We would get on a raft west of Panorama and take the exciting and refreshing trip down, ending up at Panorama village. The community of Invermere became a home community for us, and Strand's restaurant and other places became as familiar as our favourite haunts in Edmonton.

In the summertime, we enjoyed hiking in several nearby areas. We discovered a trail that led to the Lake of the Hanging Glacier, and I made that trip a few times. I believe the first or second time was with my daughter Kelly, and we have beautiful pictures of the amazing scenery on this hike. It was a strenuous climb through forest, passing a waterfall on the way, until you reached the glacial lake that is the source of Toby Creek. The ground there is covered with wildflowers, some even growing up through patches of snow on the trail.

Walking by the lake, one time, a bird flew out seemingly from beneath my foot; I had stepped on a rock with a small space beneath it where this bird had built its nest. These kinds of experiences filled me with awe, and I realized that God has created beauty all over that most of us never get to see. I felt keenly the blessing of catching these glimpses of His wonderful creation.

As I have mentioned, Panorama became not only our second home, but also a wonderful place to practice the gift of hospitality. I have no idea how many honeymoons were spent there. As word spread of this wonderful place, we had requests, sometimes from complete strangers asking if they could use the cabin. This certainly tested our assertion that this property was God's, and we had to learn how to balance hospitality with responsibility, since, as stewards of this blessing, we needed wisdom to know when to say yes and when to say no.

Panorama became a place where some special friendships were cultivated. One that comes to mind is the wonderful relationship that developed with Jack and Jo Popjes. We first got to know them when they had come home to Canada on furlough from their work with the Canela people in Brazil. They needed a place of rest to allow for a recharging of their spiritual, emotional, and physical energies. They came with us to Panorama where God used the beauty of the mountains to bring refreshment and restorative rest. The fact that God did this for them at Panorama did not surprise me, but a wonderful overflow of blessing them came with the start of a rich friendship we enjoy to this day.

After Jack and Jo became directors in Wycliffe Bible Translators, and were headquartered in Alberta, our second home became a retreat centre and a work centre for some of the Wycliffe conferences. The home was large enough to accommodate people, and the hot tub was a wonderful place to relax and enjoy the setting.

Speaking of the hot tub, we arrived at Panorama on one occasion to discover that the hot tub had disintegrated. It had inadvertently been left on when guests had departed, and the prolonged "cooking" had melted the valves, necessitating significant repairs. Even though Panorama was a place of blessing, there was always work to be done and things to be fixed. When someone isn't living in a home full time, there are a lot of things that can go wrong without the benefit of a caretaker checking in periodically.

Our friends, the Kozakaviches, had planned a period of rest and relaxation at Panorama on one occasion. Boris Kozakavich was a realtor and had, in fact, been involved in helping us find a home in Panorama, so it was a great blessing for them to be able to use the cabin. We had a birch log with holes drilled into it hanging on the main deck that served as a birdfeeder when the holes were filled with peanut butter. Before we left to return to Edmonton, we advised them to keep it filled with peanut butter so that they could enjoy watching the birds that came to feed.

Later in the week while they were watching television, they heard a tremendous racket out on the deck. They got up to look out the big windows and were amazed and slightly terrified to see a huge grizzly bear batting that birch log around while trying to get the peanut butter out. That was definitely not what they had in mind when it came to watching the birds feed! We later discovered that the grizzly bears in that area pass right through Panorama on their way down to hibernate in dens near the lake. This grizzly didn't hang around and was probably just enjoying a snack on the way to its winter sleep. I suspect the Kozakaviches didn't sleep quite so well for the remainder of the week, but when you live in nature, you get to have these experiences that, while amazing and beautiful, can be a bit disconcerting as well.

Another Panorama experience that begs to be told involved some friends who needed a time of retreat. They brought their family to Panorama for a holiday, enjoying the hiking and fishing activities while staying in the cabin. As they were cleaning up in preparation to go home, one of their sons swept up the fireplace ashes into a cardboard box which he set outside the back door. A little while later, the dad saw flickering lights outside the backdoor and went to investigate. He opened the door to find flames licking at the side of the cabin coming from the cardboard box of ashes that were apparently not completely extinguished. Water was quickly employed to put out the small blaze and disaster was averted with only a bit of charred siding to tell the story of God's protection from what could have been a more serious disaster.

When our time at Panorama came to an end, and we decided to sell our second home, we listed it and soon received a call from the realtor saying they had a prospective buyer. The buyer wanted to meet the owners and stay in the home before making a final decision. I went to Panorama and met this lovely couple from Holland. They had come to Canada and been married on a mountaintop in Banff that was only accessible by helicopter. They were a charming couple who dreamed of owning a cabin in the forest.

They were obviously well off and could afford a second home in Canada. They loved Panorama and loved our cabin. There was no haggling about the price. They bought the cabin with all of its contents and proceeded to make their home in the Invermere area. They bought up some townhomes and the top floors of some hotels, and even purchased a ranch in the vicinity. When no earthmoving equipment was available to do some work on the ranch, they even bought a caterpillar, and this cemented their reputation as the "rich people from Holland." They eventually sold "our" second home, and when we went back to see it, we discovered that much of the furniture that we had cherished had just been disposed of in favour of more modern European furnishings. They were very interesting folks.

With the sale of the home in Panorama, and the sale of our timeshares there, we decided to move out of our long- time home on 84th avenue and have a home built at 728 Ormsby Road.

31. Retirement

Retirement for Don Smailes did not mean I stopped working. It was more like getting new tires. This new chapter of life meant that I didn't need to get paid for what I did, and it also meant that I didn't have to go in to work every day at a set time. I remained active in ARS/VitalAire as part of the board but had the freedom to do other things in the day-to-day.

Retirement afforded me time to do some fishing and visiting with my brother Jerry. His home in Ontario and mine in Alberta meant that while we were both making our living, we didn't see each other as often as we might have wished. In retirement, we met for some great fishing trips in the Arctic. Jerry would bring some of his farming friends along, and we would head up north to fish for arctic char and lake trout. The fishing was great, but we also enjoyed seeing northern wildlife like muskox and caribou.

One day, we spied an animal in the distance that looked like a wolf. It was a short distance away, but we couldn't see it clearly. I picked up my binoculars to get a better look and discovered that it was a large arctic hare. My brother's friend wasn't impressed.

"Damn you, Smailes! You and your damn binoculars!! If you hadn't had those, we would have seen an arctic wolf!"

Sometime after this trip, I received a book of poetry written by this new friend. He had wonderful pictures of ptarmigan, caribou, muskox, and the twenty-five- and twenty-seven-pound lake trout and arctic char we had enjoyed. My life was enriched by these experiences and the new friendships that resulted.

On one occasion, we were above the tree line and coming over a hill to get to a lake. As we went down to the lake, we could see the ice pack in the middle, and at the edges of the lake in the clear water, there appeared to be dead trees. Since we were north of the tree line, we were puzzled to think there would be trees there.

As we began fishing, we discovered these were lake trout that were about forty pounds each! One of the fish we caught actually had another two-and-a- half-pound fish in its mouth that it was in the process of eating! The fishing here was catch and release since these fish take a long time to mature, so we used barbless hooks. If you caught a fish that you wanted as a trophy, you would take a photo of the fish and get a trophy made of Styrofoam.

I will never forget being in the lake with hip waders and chest waders. I had a fish on my line, Jerry's colleagues had fish on their lines, and Jerry's fish went around my legs and between my legs so that his line was tucked around my legs and hip waders. We managed to untangle the line so that I wouldn't be reeled in along with the fish, but we couldn't bring that particular fish in. Those were tremendous and wonderful experiences of having fun and enjoying God's amazing creation.

Another trip that I will not forget is the first trip I took with my son-in-law Marty. We went fishing at Nonacho Lake in the Northwest Territories, flying out of Hay River in a beaver or otter airplane to a fishing camp. It was one of Marty's first airplane rides as we got to know him before he and Terri were married. I found out that Marty is an avid fisherman, but we were challenged by the hordes of bugs, horseflies, and hornets that sought to distract us from fishing. It was a fun time of getting to know my amazing son-in-law, and we caught a lot of fish on that holiday.

Another fishing trip was taken with Clair and Rueben Ziolkowski and Matt, Clair's son. We went fishing off of Kitimat, BC, which boasts some of the most beautiful country you can imagine. We had rented a fishing boat that had a captain and cook to look after us. It was there that I landed my record weight salmon; I think it was forty-two or forty-four pounds. When it hit the line, I remember asking the captain, "Do we play this fish?"

"No," he answered, "you get that fish in the boat."

As soon as I could get it on the line and near the boat, he had it in a net. It was a beautiful fish that made a lot of steaks. We also enjoyed setting crab traps, and we had crab at every meal, even breakfast! The cook made a wonderful crab omelet among other tasty meals. The beauty of the ocean, and the wonder of being with friends, makes fishing so special. Each night we would camp near a natural hot spring, and we would go in to have a soak. We saw deer swim by us going from one island to another. There were eagles and osprey that fished with us, and even bears would come close to the boat. It was a wonderful experience.

Another fishing story that I will never forget was when I was a guest of Canadian Liquid Air at Peregrine Lodge in the Queen Charlotte Islands (now Haida Gwaii). VitalAire often took their clients there. I had turned down invitations to this fishing trip a number of times on prior occasions because I did not want it to influence business decisions we were to make with them. But once we had sold them 35 percent of the business, we took this trip. We flew into the Queen Charlotte Islands from Vancouver in an albatross airplane. Although we arrived at Peregrine when traditionally fishing season was at its height, they had had a couple of weeks where they were not catching any fish. People that had paid good money to be there were very disappointed.

The first time we went out, we had strikes right away, and I have never seen any fishing like this in my life. There were fish jumping six or eight feet out of the water, and they were big salmon. The king salmon were running there, and we had some of these on our lines but didn't manage to get them in the boat. It didn't take long for the guides to tell us what we were doing wrong; we needed to keep the line tight and that would keep the fish from getting off the hook.

Well, we may have been farm boys learning to fish, but we were also people who could follow instructions, and after that we never lost a fish. We ended up with the limit of fish that we could have, and it was such an amazing time. We also had some halibut that were record sized; thirty-five pounds in weight!

What I enjoyed the most was the natural setting. We were housed in an old logging camp in what used to be the staff quarters. It had been made very comfortable for us, and we had wonderful guides. It was just an amazing experience. That's what I like the most about fishing; you're out in God's wonderful nature, experiencing good fellowship with people. I have had much of this in my life and am very grateful for it.

In retirement, I soon found that I didn't know what to do with myself. I had good health, lots of energy, and an abundance of free time. Playing games and embracing a life of leisure, much as I enjoy golf and fishing, didn't fulfill me. I needed some purpose in my life. I found myself getting underfoot at home as Gerry continued with regular household chores. She certainly didn't need me to meddle with her well-tuned homemaking system.

We decided to build our retirement home and enlisted Brad

Kennedy, a family friend, to design it. Brad was a visionary whose impressive buildings can be seen throughout Edmonton. He was about to be certified as an architect when he encouraged us to dream our ideal retirement home. The result can be seen at 728 Ormsby Rd, where we lived for several happy years.

While the house was taking shape, the builders didn't need me underfoot any more than Gerry did, so I was put to work gathering stones from the building site. I enjoyed watching the carpenters work and learning what went into the construction of a home.

Gerry and I have enjoyed several cruises in retirement that have broadened our horizons. From Australia to the Mediterranean, South America, and Europe, we have been blessed to discover God's wonderful creation and the many wonderful cultures in this world of ours.

Gerry and Don on a retirement holiday

In retirement, my involvement in the church has also been significant. The relocation of Meadowlark-Westland church to become West Meadows in the current location offered a great opportunity to volunteer in my early retirement. During the initial construction of the building, a night watchman was needed to protect the building materials that were easily stolen by those involved in petty crime. I volunteered for this along with a couple of other friends. I remember one night being at the church and since there were no streetlights in the area, it was very dark. I was doing something and suddenly became aware of taillights leaving the church property. I started running towards the departing vehicle but failed to see a pile of building materials in my path because of the darkness. I made a headlong dive into terra firma, and the taillights disappeared. As I picked myself up, I began to laugh as I considered how good God was in protecting me from injury while I was not nearly so effective at protecting the construction site.

Another unforgettable incident involved the sprinkler system being installed in the new building. The church was not connected to the city water and sewer system, but instead sourced water from a dugout on the property that pumped water into the sprinkler system. During the placement of drywall on the ceiling, a tradesperson broke one of the waterspouts that would be activated in case of a fire. Water began to pour out of the ceiling until we had three feet of water at the front of the church. I was up on a ladder trying to plug the fountain of water that was flowing out of the sprinkler and almost drowned. When a truck came to pump out the water at the front of the church, something malfunctioned in his machinery, causing it to overflow even the pumper vehicle. There was water pouring out of the door and over every area and panel of the truck. It seemed like a case of baptisms starting prematurely at our church!

Another day as we were working on the church site, we noticed the police coming to the dugout. They had come with divers to try and locate something that had been buried in the dugout. It turned out to be some Chevy vehicles that had been stolen from a Chevy dealership, and the thieves had disposed of them in the dugout. I hadn't realized how deep the water was! A few of us made a sign which we posted by the dugout indicating it as the parking area for Chevy vehicles. Our pastor happened to drive a Chevy, so it was even more fun to tease him with that sign. These were wonderful opportunities to volunteer, and the friendship that developed between Ed and Rudy and me is one I cherish to this day. I love that kind of volunteering even more than the kind where you are involved in leadership.

Despite all of the advertising about the joys of not having to go to work, I found life in retirement to be somewhat boring and without purpose. I still had energy and enjoyed physical work. I began working in the community, helping neighbours with homeowner tasks like yard work, felling trees, and so forth.

When spring came and it was time to dethatch the lawn, raking up the old grass and fertilizing, I did this in my own yard, and because I was renting equipment, I simply did it for the neighbours as well while I had the equipment. It grew as God placed a desire in my heart to serve our pastors.

I remember being at Pastor Ruben's place and doing his yard. I then went next door to ask his neighbour if I could do his as well. That resulted in a great deal of wonder and gratitude from this neighbour, and as we got to know one another, I found myself praying for him. He was in a situation where his health was failing, and he was unable to do these regular homeowner duties for himself. Neither of us will soon forget praying on the sidewalk in front of his house, inviting Jesus into his situation, and then doing the work.

I discovered such joy in being able to help people that was very much like what I experienced helping people in my respiratory therapy career.

It didn't take long for me to have my eyes opened to the fact that almost every home we passed contained opportunities to bless the inhabitants simply by doing ordinary chores. It wasn't long before I had a couple of assistants. These were men who couldn't be employed in the traditional workforce, but they had capable bodies and a willingness to work. Some great friendships and ministry arose out of those connections.

Volunteering has been a big part of my retirement and I consider it a privilege to be able to serve in our community. I have always loved to cut down trees using a chainsaw. A natural outlet for my love of the outdoors and desire to help people came about when I was helping our pastors with yard work. I would do spring maintenance for them, raking up the dead grass, fertilizing the lawn, and trimming back dead trees.

One day after helping a neighbour of Matt Day, our worship pastor, with his lawn and a fence repair, Matt said, "You need a name for what you do!"

Expressions of Love became the name of this ministry—suggested by Matt when I was doing these tasks for his neighbours. Another friend, Bob Goethe III, helped us clarify why we did what we did and that was incorporated into our letterhead along with some graphics by Randy Hayashi. We decided that Expressions of Love summed up what we were doing and why we did it.

If we saw a dead tree in someone's yard and that person was not home, we would leave a note offering to remove the tree. When people called, they would ask how much we charged for tree removal. We would reply that there was no charge and ask where they would like the wood to be stacked.

Our service would be the beginning of a friendship, and we would often find that there were other needs in the family that we would help alleviate. This was not unlike our respiratory home care work where God opened doors to care for people in ways that went beyond whatever task had originally brought us to their home.

I found out that I could buy a 20 kg bag of fertilizer from the agricultural plant north of St. Albert for one-fifth of the price that it cost at the hardware store. It was better quality fertilizer, and if you purchased a half-ton of it, there was no GST charged because you were considered a farmer. They say you can take the boy off the farm, but it's harder to take the farmer out of the boy.

I still had a strong desire to help people with medical needs, so I took a course in palliative care that would enable me to volunteer in hospital.

My first assignment took me to the Charles Camsell Hospital where I visited a few patients before meeting a young man who was to become my main challenge. Ken was a giant of a man at six-foot-nine-inches. He did not walk or talk but communicated with a computer. His hands were disfigured, and he looked a bit scruffy.

I asked if I could give him a shave, and he consented. Afterwards, we played a game of cribbage, and I learned his story. He had a genetic disorder called Wilson's disease that caused him to absorb too much copper. This had a detrimental effect on his organs, eventually destroying his liver.

Further conversations as our friendship developed revealed a traumatic childhood that had left Ken emotionally crippled. His father had abandoned him at a young age, and there were areas of deep hurt in his life. After his liver transplant, Ken had decided that he would not walk or talk anymore, and that he would just let the government take care of him.

As we became friends, Ken was convinced to walk and talk again. I'm no miracle worker but having someone care about you and lay down some "rules of engagement" can make a difference in any life. Ken eventually got out of the hospital, opened a bank account, and moved home. His problems were not over, but I like to think our friendship helped persuade him to take another shot at life.

32. Timber!!

Although golf and travel occupied a good part of my retirement schedule, volunteer activities, particularly if they involved a chainsaw, were my favourite pastime. I don't know where my love for cutting down trees came from. It's not that I don't appreciate forests and trees, but I grew up in situations where trees had to be removed either to clear space for a home or garden, or because the trees were dead.

When we had our property at Panorama, I got a lot of experience cutting down trees that had beetle kill. When I retired in Edmonton, there were diseased birch trees and some spruce trees that just became too big for the space they were in. Our school system gave children in Grade 1 or 2 a tiny spruce tree to plant as part of learning about nature. After several years, these little trees would grow taller and faster than the child, often surpassing the house in height.

I remember cutting down one such tree at my friend Caroline Zeitner's house. It was a beautiful tree that had simply become too big for the yard. When I cut down the tree, we ended up with two large garbage bags of cones that had been on the tree; proof that mother nature knows how to prepare for survival of a species!

We had no place to put the branches, so I got a small trailer to pull behind my Land Cruiser. We would haul the trees and branches somewhere where they could be burnt safely. A chipper would have been useful to make all these branches into mulch, but we didn't have one. So, we hauled these spruce branches all the way out to Warburg where we could burn them in a safe place. Loading and unloading the branches gave you an appreciation for the wind protection they offered in the forest. When I had a big spruce branch in my hand, the wind would carry the branch and me with it to where I didn't necessarily want to go!

Causing a tree to fall in a particular direction is a skill I never fully mastered. The wind will blow a tree over according to the weight of the branches no matter how the trunk has been notched. To manage this, I obtained a come-along that I could connect to the tree and hitch to my vehicle. This pressure made it easier for the tree to fall where I wanted it to. The weight of a falling tree was another thing that is hard to describe if you haven't experienced it at close range.

While felling a tree on 159th Street in Edmonton, a neighbour who lived three doors down came out to see what I was doing. He said that the impact of that tree hitting the ground had caused his house to shake. Another person who was a clockmaker had to adjust all of the clocks in his repair shop since the impact of trees falling near his home had caused them to change time!

Neighbours would often come to see what I was doing since there's nothing like a chainsaw to pique the curiosity of anyone within earshot. Invariably, they would offer helpful advice, even though most of them had never felled a tree before. I learned to smile and assure them that I knew what I was doing. If the advice persisted, I would suggest they get their own chainsaw and take up this hobby!

There was a young man who helped me on occasion, and we became good friends. He was affected by a bipolar disorder and had been an ironworker. Since his previous work had been working high above the ground on ironworks, he had no fear of heights. He was a good worker, and we had a lot of fun.

The culminating event in my tree-felling "career" happened in February of 2006. I was cutting down a tree for a family friend who lived near 76th Avenue and 106th Street in Edmonton. This tree was causing all sorts of problems with our friends' fishpond. It also annoyed the neighbours who had to deal with leaves and other unwanted things dropped in their yards

I had gone up and down the ladder a few times to trim branches and secure my come-along to ensure the tree fell in the right place. I was about twenty feet up above the frozen ground, dealing with some branches that were in my way, and must have gotten careless. I had no harness on, and suddenly realized that I was falling. I released the chain saw which was running, and the next thing I knew, there was an ambulance crew taking stock of my injuries as I lay on the ground.

While I was working on the tree, my wife and friend were having coffee in the house. Apparently, a neighbour was watching from her window and saw me fall. She called our friend to let her know, and they called emergency services. When Gerry ran outside, she found me lying on my back, attempting to remove the helmet from my bloodied head. She tried to help me, and I must have been in shock because I don't remember whether I got the helmet off or not. When the ambulance crew arrived, they carefully loaded me onto a stretcher since it was likely that my back had been broken after such a fall.

In the ambulance, I was struggling to breathe, and said to the crew, "You have to turn me on my side! I can't breathe!!"

The ambulance attendant asked my wife, "How many years have you had to put up with this nonsense?"

We arrived at the university hospital where I spent the next eighteen days as a patient. I was put in the trauma unit where it was discovered I had a fractured skull, several fractured vertebrae, broken ribs, and pneumothorax. It took five days to stabilize me so that they could do surgery to repair the vertebrae.

Gerry called the kids to let them know what had happened, and they rallied around to support us. The care I received in hospital was exceptional, and I found myself wondering whether having this sort of experience prior to my career in respiratory therapy might not have made me a better healthcare provider. It certainly made me appreciate the quality of healthcare staff and the ability to move freely without pain! My pain was controlled by the frequent administration of morphine which helped with my discomfort but caused me to see things that others couldn't see. At one point I asked my son, "Why don't people pick up the oranges that are underneath that tree? I need them!!"

It was an interesting time and difficult because of the care and procedures I needed. Before my surgery, I was on spinal precautions which meant the nursing staff had to turn me periodically to avoid bedsores, but turning me was a two-person job since my spine had to be kept in alignment. When my kids were visiting me one day, Evan was seated on one side of the bed while the nurses turned me away from him. Having inherited his dad's sense of humour, he quipped, "Never thought I'd get to see the crack of dawn at this time of day!"

It was certainly a humbling time, being so helpless, and it gave me a better understanding of what it is to be a patient. It also gave me a deep appreciation for my family as they gathered around and showed their love through visits, prayers, and just being there. Evan even borrowed a guitar, and we had a bit of a worship time right there in the hospital which was wonderful.

After five days, I was taken to the OR where Dr. Mitch Lavoie and

God put me back together. My back was fused from thoracic vertebrae seven to eleven, packed with appropriate bone marrow in the right places, and titanium rods were placed on both sides of my spine. After surgery, I was taken to the ICU to recover. I developed a hemothorax after surgery and needed a chest tube.

When Gerry and my kids were allowed in to see me, I was still intubated and restrained since I had apparently tried to pull out the breathing tube when I had partially awakened earlier. When Gerry saw me, pale and with tubes coming out all over, she was a bit shocked. The reality of how serious my injuries were had perhaps not sunk in completely.

An announcement came over the PA system, and I opened my eyes. The old hospital worker habit of attending to calls over the PA system was still ingrained in my sedated brain. According to Kelly, I began to struggle with the restraints, trying to remove the breathing tube, and becoming agitated as I fought against the foreign tube down my throat. The nurse was called and administered a sedative that calmed me, but Gerry was shaken. The nurse advised that I probably wouldn't be awake and responsive until the next day, so Gerry and Kelly returned home.

I must have had another episode or two of trying to pull out the breathing tube during the evening which caused the care team to realize I should be de-intubated or taken off the ventilator and allowed to breathe on my own. They did this and called Gerry at home to tell her. The person calling her said, "We're taking your husband off life support."

Gerry was just getting ready for bed and replied that she would come to the hospital as quickly as she could. She called Terri in a panic, relaying what she had been told, and both of them thought I had deteriorated to the point where the healthcare team was going to "pull the plug."

When Gerry arrived at the hospital and found that they were taking me off the ventilator because I was ready to breathe on my own, she was tempted to strangle the nurse who had called with such a dire update. An unfortunate choice of words which caused Gerry to think I had died.

As I healed and the different tubes were removed, I was equipped with a specially fitted support jacket. It was made of a combination of hard and soft plastic and was tailored to provide support for my healing body as I moved around. The idea was to provide structure for my bones as they healed, and the muscles were strengthened to support my spine.

After eighteen days in the hospital, I was released with this jacket to continue healing at home. Two months later, I went to the hospital for a follow-up with the surgeon. X-rays were taken, and Dr. Lavoie gave me the green light to do whatever my body would allow me to do.

Several friends and neighbours advised that I should not tackle any more trees taller than a potentilla. Gerry and the kids wanted to hide or destroy my chainsaw after this incident. While grateful to God and the talented medical professionals for saving my life, I'm not sure whether the gravity of my accident had made an impression on me. I was still talking about not giving up chainsaws and climbing trees. Gerry recalls Kelly taking my face in her hands, looking into my eyes, and saying, "It's not just about you!"

33. Compassion Call

Anyone who knows me has undoubtedly been made aware of my passion for helping others. God has gifted me with strength and has entrusted me with material wealth to share. I have always recognized that I am only a steward of these resources, and my greatest joy is participating in God's kingdom through giving and serving others.

Some years ago, I was introduced to Compassion, a Christian child sponsorship organization, through my friend Len Johnson. Len sponsored a child in Colombia and was going to visit a missionary there. I decided to have him select a child for me to sponsor. Len returned with pictures of Deysi, a ten-year-old girl who became my first international correspondent. I sent letters telling Deysi about my life in Canada and received replies from this young girl. Her letters always came with brightly colored drawings, and I soon felt a deep connection with this child.

We had Colombian friends at our church, and I decided to approach them about a visit to their homeland. Gerry and I sponsored three more children in Colombia through Compassion while I made plans to accompany Carlos and Luddy Quintero to Colombia to visit these children.

The flight to Bogotá was a long one, and we arrived late on a Saturday evening. We were graciously hosted by family of the Quinteros in a loaned apartment. As our journey began, I had no idea how this trip would change my life.

On Sunday, we went to my first church service in Colombia. I did not speak Spanish, the language of the country, and was dependent on the Quinteros to translate for me.

We went to a church that was unlike any I had experienced before. The church was situated in a type of warehouse and had at least a thousand people attending the service. They had four services, one right after the other to accommodate all those who wanted to attend, and there were television screens mounted for the service so that everyone could see what was happening no matter where they were seated in this large venue.

The passion of the people and the sheer number participating in services convinced me that the country was alive with the Spirit of God. I wished that our North American churches could visit and experience worshiping with these precious Colombian believers. This wasn't a one-time event at that particular church; the experience was duplicated every Sunday during my twenty-nine-day visit to Colombia. No matter the location, there was an unmistakable excitement and zeal for the kingdom of God.

When the day for my Compassion visit arrived, I was transported to the Compassion office in Bogotá where I received a tour to see how the different programs were administered in Colombia. My mouth must have been hanging open the whole time; I have never seen such an efficient organization!

The people giving me the tour showed me how a church would apply to have a Compassion centre or child development program, and how every monetary gift down to the last penny was accounted for. A Compassion representative would visit the church regularly after the program was set up to monitor the program, children, and staff. There were regular audits, and everything was so transparent that I realized what an exceptional organization this was. There was no question that the funds we provided for our sponsored children were well administered and that the churches in charge of the programs were held accountable.

From the Compassion centre in Bogotá, we went by van to the community where Deysi's church program was located. My translator was a young man named Roberto. His command of English was excellent, and he soon told me how he became involved with Compassion.

Because he was fluent in both Spanish and English, he worked translating the letters between sponsors and children. At that time, Roberto was in a relationship with a young lady with whom he had a child. While he was busy doing his translation work, God used the messages of the children and their sponsors to make him aware of his need for Jesus. He became a follower of Jesus, married this girl that he was with, and they became a new Christian family.

By the time we reached the church where Deysi's Compassion program was located, Roberto and I had become friends.

When we arrived at the church, I was greeted as if I was the president of the United States. I could not believe the reception they gave me!

Soon, I found myself face to face with Deysi, my beautiful ten-year-old Colombian correspondent. We exchanged gifts, and I was able to meet her mom and little sister as we enjoyed lunch together. I still have the little Colombian clock that Deysi gave me that day, and it evokes wonderful memories of our first meeting.

After lunch, I found myself wrapped in a Colombian flag that was the same size as the Canadian flag I had brought for the church.

Wrapped in the Colombian flag, hugging Deysi

We played some games with the other children in the church and outside on the sports field. I was so impressed with how Deysi shared with the younger children. After a number of games and some other activities, it was time for the kids to go home.

I was able to walk Deysi home, and, as we walked, she made me aware of every dog that couldn't be trusted and the ones that could. She was very attentive and careful, watching out for her foreign visitor.

We came to her home, a modest apartment, where her mother and little sister greeted us. Her dad was not there, but I got a tour of the home, and we were served a lovely meal. Seeing the room which Deysi shared with her little sister was not what I expected. There were books on a shelf and a number of small stuffed animals. Everything in their home was clean and seemed quite adequate. I may have been anticipating a greater degree of poverty, but theirs was a well-established home with love and simple things that appeared to meet their needs. The Compassion program was certainly a help for Deysi and her family as they sought to make the most of any opportunity to improve the health and well-being of their children.

Too soon, it was time to walk back to the church and complete our day together. Deysi asked about my wife and wondered why she was not with me. She obviously wanted to meet her. We saw a school child coming home from classes with a backpack, and I asked Deysi if she had a backpack like that.

"Sure," she said. "You bought me one."

As we passed blooming roses, I remember saying how much my wife Gerry enjoyed roses. Deysi wanted to send some roses back for Gerry, but of course that was not possible. Too soon, we arrived back at the church, realizing our visit was over. It had been an amazing day full of new experiences and a deepening of our sponsor and child relationship.

We hugged and said our goodbyes, hoping that we would be able to see each other again. Even if another meeting wasn't possible, I knew we would be forever connected at a heart level.

Returning to my lodgings at the end of that full day, I retired to my sleeping quarters for a time of reflection. Whatever else happened during the remainder of my stay in Colombia, I would love to spend another day at this Compassion centre. I wanted to just serve the pastor and walk Deysi home and back. I didn't know that I would have that opportunity later on.

A few days later, Compassion had arranged for me to go and see the other three children we were sponsoring in Colombia. I boarded a plane to Medellin, the Compassion project there where we sponsored Jhonathan and Tatiana.

When I reached the church that administered the Compassion program in that area, I was introduced to Jhonathan and Tatiana. Jhonathan was in Grade 4, and it was obvious that he had a very good relationship with the Compassion staff. Tatiana was a shy, beautiful girl of African heritage. She was so timid that we didn't have the same connection I had experienced with Deysi.

Jhonathan was very excited and outgoing and could already speak some English which he was anxious to practice with me. Compassion had arranged a translator to help fill in the gaps in our communication abilities.

We visited Jhonathan's home which was very near the church in a densely populated area. We were introduced to his parents, and they welcomed me as family. His dad was a shoemaker, and before I left their home, I had been measured for a pair of handmade shoes. It's hard to describe the love and appreciation that one felt as a sponsor.

Meeting Jhonathan for the first time

When we returned to the church, we looked down the mountain a half-mile or so, to Jhonathan's school. Jhonathan wanted me to come to his school, and I soon found myself in front of a class of nine-year-olds, talking about my impressions of Colombia. I felt like a Canadian ambassador to Colombia as I shared through an interpreter how much I loved Colombia, especially the people.

There was no question of Jhonathan's scholastic ability and his leadership, even as a nine-year-old in school. And there was no sense of dissatisfaction among the students. They all seemed happy to be there, and I was the "celebrity," but a very humbled one as God was dealing in my heart. I was keenly aware of the beauty of this country and of the tremendous privilege I had to be there. The day was soon over, but it was unforgettable.

The next day found me on a small twenty-six-seater aircraft, heading to Magangue in the northern part of Colombia. Arriving at the airport, I was greeted by people who took me to the project where Maria was a student. After giving us something to eat, the children performed wonderful cultural dances in a program for me.

The pastor of this church centre was herself a graduate of the Compassion program! I had such wonderful conversations with her and with her mentors. Again, we had a time of exchanging gifts with Maria and her family. A relative of Maria was a glassworker, and I was given a beautiful glass book stand for my Bible which I packed carefully so that it would survive the trip home.

That night, I was housed in a hotel and as I looked out over the city after the full day, I was tired but so content. Everything I could possibly have needed had been provided for me. I went to sleep and on waking in the morning discovered that the pastor's husband had kept watch outside my door all night long just to make sure I was able to rest safely and undisturbed.

As I remember these events, my eyes fill with tears at the beauty and wonder of what God was working in my heart, causing me to fall in love with Compassion. I went out on my balcony and was amazed to see families of five people on a motorcycle as the dad would be taking his children to school, and I just realized that I was in a very special place.

The next morning, I was taken back to the airport after wonderful discussions with the pastor and her mentors in the church. Due to thunderstorms and unsettled weather, my flight was delayed until it was safe.

On the trip back to Medellin, as I pondered the view from the windows of that little plane, I thought about Len Johnson's role in introducing me to Compassion and felt the Lord ask if I would be willing to represent Compassion like he had when I returned to Canada. Of course, I answered "Yes!" How could I not after such a life changing experience?

When I returned to Medellin, Carlos and Luddy had come there because we were to be guests in the home of a professor of engineering at the local university. His wife was a physician in that community. They took us to their apartments where they had rental suites, and we enjoyed a wonderful time of meditation together. What a beautiful city! The educational centre in the mountains provided a revelation of the adversity that Colombia had experienced. This doctor and engineer had been befriended by Carlos and Luddy when they came to the University of Alberta to teach and receive further engineering training. We were welcomed as family, and I was unofficially adopted by them.

Don with Luddy and Carlos Quintero in Colombia

After spending about a week in Medellin, we travelled by bus to Cali. It was an unforgettable trip. We travelled at night on the bus, and as we looked out the windows, we saw sheer drop offs of about a mile down and were grateful for the skill and ability of the bus drivers to maneuver that road safely, trip after trip. Our time in Cali was amazing, but my heart was back in Bogotá, in the little community where Deysi and her family lived.

When we arrived back in Bogotá, I received the news that I could spend another day with Deysi, her mother, and sister at a nearby tourist area. Deysi and her family arrived early in the morning, and we proceeded by bus to the tourist centre. I didn't realize that they had already spent an hour and a half on public transit to get to Bogotá, but they didn't complain as we travelled to the exhibition area. This was a special amusement park where the life and culture of Colombia was on display.

When we arrived, we saw horses and Brahma bulls, cattle, pigs, and dogs, all of them performing tricks and showing off their abilities. There was a small chameleon lizard that mesmerized us by its ability to blend into any background. We put it on Deysi's shirt and took a picture. Deysi and her sister got to ride on the Brahma bulls and on the ponies. We got to milk cows and feed little piglets with bottles.

The day was just full of these activities. As we sat by a little pond having our lunch, we saw a mother duck out on the water with her mate. I said to Deysi, "That mother duck has a nest somewhere, and I think we can find it."

We went to the little bush area by the water and found a nest full of duck eggs hidden beneath some feathers. This reminded me of my heritage growing up in Canada when I had raised ducks for a while on the farm in Beatty. We enjoyed watching the dogs do tricks and the cowboys showing off the culture of Colombia on horseback. It was absolutely amazing.

We walked through some rose gardens that formed part of the park, and Deysi, remembering my wife Gerry's fondness for roses, said that she would love to send some roses to her.

At the end of the day, we took the bus back to Bogotá where I said goodbye to the translator and to Deysi and her family. They still had an hour-and-half journey ahead of them to get home, and it was already evening. It had been a wonderful day, full of God's presence that had cemented forever the relationship I had with Deysi and her family. This little girl held a special place in my heart, and I was so glad that this was not the last time we saw each other.

When I returned to Edmonton, I volunteered as an advocate with Compassion. I was able to share in various churches and even on the radio about my experience in Colombia. Compassion had tables at different events and concerts as well where I had the privilege of helping people connect with sponsoring a child. Our personal sponsorship increased as well when God laid on my heart the desire to sponsor in other areas of Compassion. We began to sponsor a child under the child survival program in Bolivia and then also had the privilege of sponsoring a young woman in the Dominican Republic in the Leadership Development Program.

*Don and
Gerry with
Milca in the
Dominican
Republic*

Milca was studying medicine, and we were able to sponsor her through university and even to attend her graduation from the program as she became a physician.

Since that first trip to Colombia, I had opportunity to go to Guatemala with my nephew Clair Ziolkowski where we sponsored two more children with Compassion. A trip to El Salvador with the Greenfield Community Church provided the chance to visit a child that my niece was sponsoring and to deliver some gifts on her behalf.

Gerry and I took a trip to the Dominican Republic to meet several of our sponsored children and were overwhelmed by the hospitality of these families that had very little materially, yet shared their hearts with us so extravagantly. One of our sponsored boys there, Angel, had dreams of playing baseball, and I was able to entrust him with my well-used treasured ball glove. Both Gerry and I felt so loved and honoured by the kids and their families as we visited them and saw what Compassion was doing in the area.

Don and Gerry visiting Compassion in the Dominican Republic

Several years later, Kelly was able to accompany me on another trip to Colombia to visit our sponsored children there. I got to connect again with Deysi, Jhonathan, and Tatiana, and see how they had grown into wonderful young people on the cusp of adulthood.

Don and grown-up Deysi in Colombia, 2013

Sharing the experience with my daughter enriched both of our lives and added a special memory to our relationship. Investing some of God's fiscal abundance into the lives of children has brought amazing transformation to my own life, and I'm so grateful for the opportunities God has given me to experience His kingdom in other countries. One of my favourite volunteer activities is sharing the work of Compassion in various churches and venues, seeking to see more people embrace the opportunity to sponsor children with this amazing organization.[6]

34. Touchmark and Expressions of Love

After my life altering fall in 2006 and the resulting fractures to my back, ribs, and skull, I took some time to recuperate. Although Gerry and I still loved our retirement home at 728 Ormsby Rd, we wondered whether it might be time to look at other living arrangements better suited for our aging bodies.

One day while driving down Lessard Road, we saw a sign saying that a retirement community was to be built where there had previously been an abandoned farm. This piqued our interest, and we stopped in at the bungalow office for some details. Within a day or two, we had people sitting at our kitchen table, talking to us about investing in this new venture and becoming residents of the community. We moved into the retirement community of Touchmark at Wedgewood a short time later.

The Touchmark community faced challenges as it sought to make profits for its shareholders, while still providing necessary services for the residents. As in many organizations, there weren't sufficient resources to look after everything. I remember sitting in meetings and hearing complaints about how litter around the property wasn't being picked up. I felt God's Spirit nudge me, saying, "You could do that. A little humility never hurt anyone!"

I began to pick up the garbage from the garbage rooms and put it in the compactor. I soon discovered that there were a lot of recyclable bottles being disposed of, so I added bottle collection to my job description. I would collect the bottles, clean them up, and take them to the bottle depot. The revenue from the bottles went into the staff Christmas fund to reward our dedicated staff who served us so well.

This was another instance to show me that service is not related to prestige, but that it is based on what needs to be done. The rewards of friendship with the staff at Touchmark and the bottle depot became a testimony to the fact that when Jesus calls us to do something, no matter how seemingly small, the results are very fulfilling.

During this time, my daughter Terri was working for Jasper Place

Health and Wellness Centre. This was a ministry to people who found themselves in need of help in many areas from housing to healthcare to employment and income support. The facility served as a drop-in centre where those who needed assistance could come to access supports.

Someone had been picking up unsold groceries from the store across the road from our home to take them to the centre for the people there, but due to health reasons, they were unable to continue doing this. Terri asked if I would go to the store to see if the food was still available, and, if so, to deliver it to the centre twice a week.

When I went to the store to meet the manager, I discovered that with the amalgamation of Safeway and Sobeys, this store had become somewhat of a surplus store. There was a great deal of uncertainty among the staff, including the manager, about whether they would still have jobs after all the dust cleared. It seemed like a wonderful opportunity for a former entrepreneur to get involved.

When I went to see the loading dock, I saw that there were an awful lot of groceries that could be used by the less fortunate instead of going to waste. I felt like God was saying the secret was to make friends with those at the store, serve the store, and see what I could do to help the situation. That was not a difficult assignment for an ambitious senior. Not only was there enough stuff to pick up twice a week, there was enough surplus to warrant a daily pickup.

It wasn't long before we had a pickup service happening six days per week, taking surplus food to nearby schools and setting up depots in local churches. We had enough for the Jasper Place Centre, Hope Mission, and more. I immediately thought this would be a great ministry to be housed in local churches, but the churches that we contacted did not see this as part of their program. The churches did, however, become a source for more volunteers.

This opportunity to serve by transporting excess food from our local Co-Op store to various inner-city organizations proved a great alternative to my former activities with the chainsaw. It was a win-win situation as I saw it: the store could avoid food waste by sending produce and other items that could no longer be sold to people who were most grateful to receive these items. I met people who were afflicted by psychological problems, addictions, out of work, and who were just needing a little help.

The best volunteers, in my opinion, came from friends in our retirement community. They were not only wonderful volunteers with time to devote to this endeavour, they also had life experience skills. This waste prevention "business" continued to grow to the point where it almost became a full-time job which was not necessarily what any of the volunteers were able or willing to commit to.

God's leading to serve the store opened up tremendous friendships with the staff at the store. People would come in for no other reason than to serve, and those friendships continue to this day. The shipper receiver became a very good friend and began to call us the PW (Preventing Waste) crew.

Preventing waste was wonderful, but the friendships were even better. When this shipper receiver was getting married, we volunteers were invited to his wedding. Even after our volunteer service ended, the friendship continued, and we were able to take this man to his eye clinics when he suffered a detached retina.

In serving one of the local schools in Ormsby, we took over delivery of some goods from the store that had previously been picked up by the teachers. Since we were going to the store every day to pick up goods for other organizations, it only made sense that we could save these teachers the trip.

It was such a delight to see the children and how the school volunteers and staff served the community. In the summer when school is out, we discovered that there was still a childcare program operating out of the school. Providing them with food from the store was like serving at the United Nations. We discovered that our neighbourhood was made up of many people who had come to Canada from all over the world. What a joy it was to interact with these young people and find out where they had lived before Canada.

Lest one believe that the life of a volunteer retiree was all positive, I have to confess that there was a downside. In the course of my community grocery deliveries, I collected three traffic tickets with significant fines. They say no good deed goes unpunished; however, if I'm honest I must admit that I've always had somewhat of a heavy foot. God is obviously still dealing with me, and I'm trying to learn whatever lesson is intended through this experience.

Another opportunity came my way when the life enrichment director at Touchmark became of aware of a program called Capital City

Cleanup. I've always been very capable of making a mess; just ask my wife! So, the reasonable antidote might be picking up messes left by other people. In springtime, I would pick up the debris that had collected over the winter in the properties close to Touchmark and the surrounding ravines. I've had the privilege of picking up many of the political signs left by our aspiring public servants, as well as all sorts of other litter. Some springs I had as many as twenty bags of garbage from the area between Anthony Henday Drive and 62nd Avenue. It was good exercise and before long, a colleague joined in the fun.

My activities attracted the attention of some people in the area, and a journalist wrote a column featuring a photo of me picking up trash. Then, a student from NAIT did a video documentary about Expressions of Love for his studies that further increased my notoriety.

"Love to me is self-sacrifice and service in action. It's what I do, and what I do has to come from what's in my heart. The most satisfaction I've had in life is loving people and doing something for them."[7]

Another notable retirement adventure occurred in the spring of 2019, after having hip replacement surgery. I was very fortunate to have the procedure done right before the COVID pandemic shut things down in our country. My surgery was probably one of the last ones done before non-emergency surgeries were postponed in order to care for the growing number of patients affected by COVID.

While convalescing at home, I heard that there was a need for cherry pickers in the Okanagan since most of the regular migrant workers were unable to cross the border due to pandemic restrictions. I obtained medical clearance and spousal clearance to go and pick cherries. I called the BC fruit growers to find out how I might fit into the labour force. They gave me the names of people who owned cherry orchards in the area, and I began calling them to offer my services.

"I want to come and pick cherries," I began. "I don't need to be paid; I just want to come and help with the harvest. I'm eighty-two."

There was usually a little pause on the other end of the phone line while this information was absorbed. Many of the orchards are owned by people of East Indian heritage, and most of those I spoke with didn't believe an eighty-two-year-old could handle the rigours of cherry picking. However, one man replied, "Well, you come out here and call me when you get here."

I arrived in Kelowna and went to a motel I had stayed at on other occasions. To my dismay, I found out that the $75-per-night fee I remembered had doubled to $150 because of the season. This gave me pause as I wondered whether I could afford to pick cherries for free while laying out this kind of money on lodging. I headed down to the Oliver area and stopped at the place I intended to begin picking. A senior gentleman came out, took one look at me, and said, "We don't need any cherry pickers." I had the distinct impression that he was afraid this eighty-two-year-old wasn't up to the challenge. I went across the road to the fruit packing plant and was told that if I continued on south of town, I could find someone who might let me pick their cherries.

I went to the suggested orchard and sure enough, they allowed me to pick cherries. I picked for about three hours and took the pails I had filled to the owners. "Where can I pick now?" I asked. They were concerned about having an old guy picking in the heat of the day and replied, "We have no more cherries for you to pick."

So, I got in my vehicle and drove through the beautiful countryside, ending up back at the first orchard that had declined my offer to work. There was a sign at the entrance saying, "Cherry Pickers Needed." I went down the road a little way where I met some people who said, "Yes, you can pick! Go into the orchard and here's a pail." My fellow pickers were from Mexico, and they knew how to pick cherries. They helped me to find the best tree and provided me with a pouch for picking. This meant I didn't have to hold a pail in one hand or find a branch to hang a pail from. Having both hands free made me a much better cherry picker! We used a twelve-foot ladder, and my new friends showed me how to find the best spot on the tree to set up the ladder. Up and down the ladder we went, picking cherries and doing our best to communicate. My cherry-picking colleagues spoke Spanish and some broken English, and I was wishing for an interpreter as we stumbled along with gestures and pantomime. They had Biblical names like Joshua and Caleb, which together with the beauty of my surroundings made me wonder whether I had reached the Promised Land. I marvelled at God's creation, enjoying the breeze blowing through the leafy canopy that sheltered both cherries and cherry picker. The rest of the day flew by as I enjoyed being useful and making new friends; talk about heaven for an old farm boy!

After picking from 7:00 a.m. until 7:00 p.m., I decided to forgo the two-hundred-dollar-per-night local lodging in favour of a visit with my sister Pat and her family in Kelowna. I was able to share some of the fruits of my labour, given to me by the grateful orchard owners, and we relished the biggest, juiciest cherries I had ever tasted. Turns out, these were not the cherries you would normally buy in the grocery store, but they were generally exported to China and Japan where they were sold for a better price.

After a good night's rest, I returned to Edmonton where a follow-up with my doctor confirmed that cherry picking had provided excellent rehab for my new hip.

35. The Best Crop We Ever Raised

While God allowed me to experience much affirmation and success in my career, and in retirement, what brings the most joy as I reflect on my life is the blessing of family. Looking back on my upbringing, and the heartache of loss as we scrabbled to survive as a family, I can appreciate the miracle of what God has allowed me to enjoy as a dad to my own family.

Psalm 126:5,6 says, "Those who sow with tears will reap with songs of joy. Those who go out weeping, carrying seed to sow, will return with songs of joy, carrying sheaves with them."

Having been raised in an agricultural setting, the concept of planting and harvesting is a familiar metaphor. And while I never owned a farm, I've been involved in growing a lot of crops. One can do their best to till the soil and plant good seed, but the growth of a harvest is the work of God. In much the same way, the best crop I personally got to participate in raising was my family.

Even sixty-two years later, I am amazed at God's goodness in joining together Geraldine Ziolkowski and Don Smailes, and the resulting blessing of having children. These are among the most significant events in my life.

I often say that God gives children as much to teach the parents as anything. While we have a responsibility to raise our kids, we need to be aware that they are teaching us as well. I've learned much more from observing and participating in the lives of our three children than I ever expected. I am keenly aware of my failures and am so thankful for the joy they have brought to my life.

As mentioned earlier, our firstborn taught us much as new parents and introduced us to the process of raising children. We enjoyed watching Kelly's musical talents blossom and lead to band and choir trips to different places. As she sought God's calling in her life, she worked with Youth With A Mission (YWAM) and ended up spending several years in Mexico. We enjoyed the opportunity to visit and support her as she worked there. Later, she became involved with YWAM's

School of Worship and spent some time on staff in Hawaii where we also enjoyed a visit. Eventually, she returned to Canada and while our visits are not as exotic, we do enjoy having her nearby for family celebrations.

Terri's journey took a different path as she developed administrative talents and strengths in business that led her to a career in ARS/VitalAire. Each of our children at one time worked in the business of respiratory home care, but Terri moved beyond summer projects and part-time delivery jobs into a full-time career as the executive secretary of ARS/VitalAire. I really did not want to be the boss of any of our kids in their work environment, but with Terri being the only administrative assistant and secretary for those of us in management, I was one of her bosses.

One day, in the presence of other office staff, I lost my temper and proceeded to express my displeasure with something she had done. My angry outburst was unprofessional and hurtful, but I didn't stop to think about this until the Spirit of God convicted me on the way up the stairs back to my office. I knew that what I had done was wrong, and further understood that when one sins in public, a public confession is appropriate. With tears in my eyes, I went back down the steps to ask my daughter's forgiveness. As I confessed my wrongdoing, the experience not only helped change me, but it also made an impression on the other people in the office. They knew that what I had done was wrong, but the idea that the boss should ask forgiveness and admit to being wrong in public was definitely out of the ordinary.

Terri went on to be the executive secretary/administrative assistant for the salesforce and was a valued part of the ARS/VitalAire team. During this time, Martin Wagner came into our family, marrying Terri and becoming our much-loved son-in-law. This was the first wedding of our children, and I remember standing at the back of the church with the nervous bride-to-be. As Terri took my arm, we decided to pretend we were in line for the chair lift at Panorama to dispel some of the nuptial jitters.

Getting to know Marty as a bonus son has been wonderful, and we have enjoyed some great fishing and golfing and family times together. Watching Terri and Marty build a family together has been a wonderful gift, and we've been blessed by the opportunities to be involved in their lives.

Marty's job and strong work ethic allowed Terri to be at home with the children when they came along, and Gerry and I loved watching them grow into amazing parents. They provided our first grandparent gig which has turned out to be our favourite job of all.

When Terri was pregnant with their first child, we had fun comparing bellies before she gave birth in May of 1991. We knew life would never be the same. I was in Toronto on business and hurried back to meet my granddaughter. Terri was radiant with the glow of new motherhood, and the baby was a perfect bundle of pink. The unique experience of watching your child become a parent is hard to describe. Certainly, the birth of a baby is a miracle no matter what, but having a grandchild (or six!) expands the heart in ways we could not have imagined.

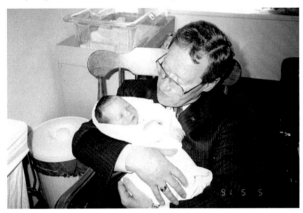

First-time grandpa

Our granddaughter grew and delighted us with many firsts as we learned the finer points of peek-a-boo, tea parties, and which Christmas ornaments we were allowed to touch on the holiday tree.

A couple of years later in October of 1993, our second granddaughter made her entrance into the world and more than doubled our joy as grandparents. Terri and Marty's home in St. Albert and then in Edmonton was the site of many birthday parties and play dates where Gerry and I got to embrace games inspired by the Beatrix Potter stories and lots of imagination.

These little girls grew into accomplished young women, pursuing careers in nursing and teaching. The fact that both of them have married wonderful young men and established their own homes and families is such a blessing. We have even been promoted to great-grandparents! What an embarrassment of blessings God has poured out on us!

Evan's journey of graduating from high school and choosing to become a respiratory therapist was another great experience in our parenting and journey as a family. When he decided he wanted to go into respiratory, he chose a three-year program in Kamloops, BC at Cariboo College. He excelled in his studies which culminated not only in graduation and registration with the Canadian Association of Respiratory Therapists but also in winning the gold medal for the highest academic honours in the registry exam. We were delighted with this news and proud as any parents would be when he received the medal at a special ceremony in Victoria.

Before going to school in Kamloops, Evan had begun dating Leanne Lebsack, and they were engaged during his first year of studies. They married the next year while Evan was still in Kamloops, and Leanne was an integral support to him as he finished his certificate and began working. They spent some time in Burnaby for a respiratory internship, then moved to Drumheller for work.

They soon discovered a definite preference for the Okanagan rather than the Badlands or prairies in Alberta, and ended up settling in Kaleden, near Penticton, BC, where they bought their first home.

In November of 1993, Evan and Leanne became parents for the first time, and we were excited to meet our first grandson. Leanne was aglow with the joy of new motherhood—I don't know if there is anything lovelier than a new mom and baby! Looking back at the photos, I am struck by how young everyone looks and amazed that such inexperienced people are entrusted with caring for a newborn.

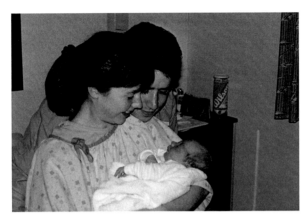

*Young,
first-time
parents,
Leanne and
Evan*

Evan and Leanne did just fine learning on the job, as we had done when faced with our own crash course in parenting. In fact, they probably did even better than we did! And, as grandparents, Gerry and I could fuss and coo over our grandchildren, offering much unsolicited advice, and then leave the parents to take charge of the more taxing activities of child rearing.

Evan and Leanne had three more visits from "the stork" over the following years, providing more precious grandkids for us to love. We had to share these grandchildren with another set of grandparents and weren't able to see them as often as the Edmonton grandkids due to distance and life responsibilities. We cherished these visits all the more as we watched them grow and develop.

We have special memories of each of our grandchildren as we sought to be as involved as we could with visits, playtime, celebrations, and cheering them on as they explored areas of interest and ability. Music, dance, cadets, biathlon, sports, and flying; such a diversity of talents!

Now as they are grown up, we are so proud of each of them as they are pursuing jobs and talents, making families of their own and growing into people that we love and cherish. I marvel at the goodness of God to our family and sometimes feel like the gospel writer who said that the world could not contain all the stories that could be told. (John 21:25)

36. Conclusion

Life is a precious gift. I have just celebrated my eighty-fifth birthday in the company of my wife, children, grandchildren, and great-grandchildren. While I had no decision about entering this world, I have been given the privilege of living a full and productive life. As I reflect on God's goodness to me and His transformation of my life, I am grateful. God has used many people to enrich my life, and I think it is fitting to share these stories.

I've returned to Beatty a few times in recent years to catch up with family and old friends, and to bid farewell to others. Although my current circumstances are a far cry from those I lived as a boy all those years ago growing up in Beatty, some things haven't changed at all. I still rely on the kindness of neighbours, still marvel at God's creation, and love to experience new things. There's still some getting into mischief, and I endeavour to stay active helping out where I can to make the world around me better. I'm keenly aware of the care and provision of God; He has been so good to me. As I reflect on His love and goodness, I realize that it's not such a long way from Beatty.

37. Acknowledgements

Just as no life is lived without the love and support of friends and family, this story has been shaped by many wonderful people.

Huge thanks to those who served as early readers. Terri Wagner, Lorraine Broz, Jennah Smailes, and Rudi Radke provided invaluable insights, suggestions, corrections, and encouragement that made the story better.

Thank you to all those who shared photos including Peter Doell, the Beatty Historical Society, Ralph Sperry, the Pearl family cousins, and extended Smailes and Ziolkowski family.

Thanks to our wonderful Pearl family relatives in the Beatty area and beyond for sharing Uncle Clifford Pearl's memories, as well as for hosting us in Beatty while we poked around researching for this book.

Thanks to Kelly Ditmars for encouragement, insight, advice, and virtual writing dates that helped get words on the page.

Thanks to Mom (Gerry Smailes) who not only lived this story, but also kept the storytellers fed and cared for, listening to every draft and idea while the book was taking shape.

Heartfelt thanks to all those who have lived this story with us. Your company along the way has made the journey so much richer.

Notes

[1]   Billy Boyd and His Cowboy Ramblers, "Tell Me Why My Daddy Don't Come Home," October 12, 1941, RCA Victor, Shellac, 10", 78 RPM.

[2]   Homer Rodeheaver and Oswald J. Smith, "Then Jesus Came," 1940. Listen to a recording of the late George Beverly Shea singing this lovely hymn for a real treat!

[3]   Larry Christenson, The Christian Family, Bloomington: Bethany House Publishers, 1970.

[4]   The article can be found in Canadian Inhalation Therapy 1, no. 3 (Fall 1965).

[5]   The article can be found in Canadian Inhalation Therapy 2, no. 4 (December 1966): 1.

[6]   For more information about Compassion Canada,
see https://www.compassion.ca.
Or in other countries:
https://www.compassion.com/

[7]   Don Smailes quote in documentary by NAIT student. Myles Belland, Expressions of Love, Dec 30, 2014, https://vimeo.com/115668731.